THE
Crowded
Nest
SYNDROME

Surviving the Return of Adult Children

KATHLEEN SHAPUTIS

Other books by Kathleen Shaputis
"Grandma Online" (Ten Speed Press)

Library of Congress Cataloging-in-Publication Data

Shaputis, Kathleen.

The crowded nest syndrome : surviving the return of adult children / by Kathleen
Shaputis.— 1ˢᵗ ed.

        p. cm.
ISBN 0-9726727-0-2 (pbk. : alk. paper)
1. Parent and adult child. I. Title.
HQ755.86.S533 2003
306.874—dc21
        2003005595

First Edition, July 2003

Clutter Fairy Publishing
Olympia WA 98508-1056

Cover Design by Kathy Campbell

Book Designed and Printed in the United States of America
by Gorham Printing, Rochester, WA
www.GorhamPrinting.com

Distributed by Independent Publishers Group (800) 888-4741

The Crowded Nest Syndrome

To my dad

Who's been there for me from the beginning
applauding, laughing, and loving

Acknowledgements

Surviving CNS means having a great support team around you and I have one of the best. This book has been a labor of love and I owe a debt of thanks and gratitude for the encouragement of many incredible individuals, not the least of which is the president of my fan club and keeper of my heart, Jean Butera.

Among the team are a few CNS sufferers including Colleen, my California rock; Kay, fellow author and confidant; Richard, who came down with CNS the same year I did and always had stories to brighten my day; and the infamous coupon queen, Carolyn.

My non-CNS team members could fill a football stadium. Some are writers, moms, relatives, but all are terrific people. Their friendship and dedication over the years mean a lot. A brief few from that long list include Tana, Lola, Lee, Becky, Doreen, and Shani.

Family support is another California link in my support bracelet. From big brothers Jim and Bob, as well as big sister Sherry, with special gratitude going to Aunt Fran.

I'd like to thank my editor, Bev Stumpf, of B Write Services, Issaquah, Washington. She, too, is a fellow CNS sufferer.

Behind every great book is a production staff that rarely gets its true recognition. Kurt and Norma Gorham, of Gorham Printing in Rochester, Washington are book printers extraordinare. They've combined a talented team of employees any author would love to work with, including their outstanding graphic designer, Kathy Campbell, and the quality press production of Dan and Del.

This book would not have been possible, of course, without the family members that started it all—husband, Bob, and defender of the rest of them; Brian, Jamie, the infamous Joshua James, incorrigible Isaiah, and newest addition, Little Joe. I may whine and moan about this crew, but somebody's gotta love em.

Contents

CROWDED NEST SYNDROME

Introduction

Just when you thought it safe to pop the cork on the magnum of champagne squirreled away in the dark recess of the refrigerator to celebrate your official empty nest, here they come trudging back home. Overgrown rug rats in adult clothing. Tall toddlers you raised with sweat and tears for over two decades of 24/7 motherhood, set free into the world as independent people, back home again. Who knew? The fresh coat of paint hasn't dried on the walls of your new office or exercise room, when these "Boomerang" kids show up demanding their old rooms be returned to them in original condition.

Adult children are moving back in with their parents at alarming rates in the 21st century bringing extra baggage with them. Not designer-label kinds, mind you, but the damaged-emotional-duffle-bag kind. This epidemic of frightening proportions is afflicting many baby boomers in America today. For every two or three children who mature into successful, independent young adults, there is one who can't quite get it together and comes home to Mama. The latest U. S. Census data reports one out of four (27%) 18 to 34-year-olds are living with their parents. (The author respectfully requests permission to live at one of those other three homes. Please.) These young people are classified as the Boomerang Generation—always coming back to the place they started.

A year or two earlier these young people were probably enjoying independent adulthood. They hadn't given a thought to coming home, but suddenly find they are no longer able to cope, financially or emotionally, and have no place else to turn. Boomerang kids present unique problems since they once functioned on their own; they've tasted free-range living as an adult—and liked it.

Granted the national economy is causing problems with skyrocketing housing costs dampening the spirit of new independents. But when hasn't it? Monthly rent on a dilapidated studio apartment in any large metropolitan area (cockroaches and other vermin included) is almost a full month's paycheck. Sound familiar? How many of us got creative back in the Sixties and Seventies using particleboard and cinder blocks for furniture, surviving a revolving door of roommates? Blaming the economy problems on current Republicans or Democrats, depending on your affiliation, will not get your peace and quiet back once the Boomerangs move in. In fact bringing up current events may incite them to panic and hunker into the homestead security even more.

Don't count on marrying them off (as if that's a cheaper solution) to get them out from under foot. With the typical age of a first marriage rising into the mid-twenties, kids are staying home longer. This gives them more time to sit around and figure out how to create a twenty- or thirty-thousand-dollar wedding extravaganza. Add the fact there is a fifty percent divorce rate and even the expensive postponed marriages crash and burn quickly. Suddenly you find the broken hearted adult child on your doorstep, again, with an Espresso machine under his or her arm.

Things happen, into every life a little rain must fall, yadda, yadda. Pick a bumper sticker slogan. The backwash of a failed marriage or bouts of financial strain from corporate layoffs may create brief (and the author stresses the word brief) respites when young adults need our support to lick their wounds at home before jumping back into the realm of harsh reality. No one said being a parent was only an eighteen-year commitment. They stay a few months, it was nice seeing them again, you say, "Have a nice life," and poof, they're gone.

However, hordes of Seinfeld-wanna-be's don't have a clue how irresponsible they've become. After an initial period meant to pick themselves up, these over-aged children start enjoying home a bit too much. Meet the Boomerang Buttheads, millions of young men and women who are sneaking back to their parents' home because of disastrous personal choices. A choice such as too many turns riding the credit card carousel and racking up horrendous financial debt.

In this book I may refer to returning adult children as RAC's or just the term Boomerang from the Boomerang Generation. I could call my own a few other choice words, but I'd have to wash my mouth out with soap.

Boomerangs don't want the responsibility of struggling back to economic independence, just the privileges of adulthood they've grown accustomed to—cable television, long distance phone service, a hot meal on the table, and clean laundry every week as only Mom provides. Extending their stays at the parental homestead to bask in adolescent security blankets is their theme, which translated means using and abusing Mom's house, Mom's checkbook, and Mom's car.

These Generation X, Y, & Zers conveniently forget to make plans to get back out on their own. "Where else can I get free rent, a stocked refrigerator, cable TV, and my laundry done?" is an attitude of many young adults. For them the $64,000 question is not, "Why do I live at home again," but "Why would I live anywhere else?"

When this happens, you need to stand up and help them take that first step toward independence. Take action. Start by reading this helpful tome, then hit them up along the side of their head with the book, drop it on their stocking feet propped up on your coffee table for the gazillionth time, or lean it against the empty carton of orange juice in the refrigerator. Magic mirror on the wall—show me the Boomerang down the hall.

Know your enemy, you gave birth to them.

Kathleen Shaputis
March 2003

CROWDED NEST SYNDROME

1

Detach Yourself: Then the Phone, TV . . .

The definition of the word *detach* in Webster's dictionary is "separate and survive." Oops, sorry, that's my definition. Good ol' Noah Webster didn't have adult children invading his house the moment after he and his wife got it set up for easy, breezy, no-more-children-at-home living. Though, actually, his definition is fairly relevant for having been coined back in 1686.

> *De-tach: to separate, especially from a larger mass*
> *and usually without violence or damage.*

I love the part about "without violence or damage." You used to be able to swat a toddler on the diaper when they misbehaved—a quick attention grabber decades before the words "time out" became the punishment of choice. As your hand connected with the plastic-coated tushy, your mouth was firmly saying "no." Those were the early days when you thought you had control over the little darlings. Giving them a swat on the diapered end was a safety precaution when they were trying to do something that would hurt themselves or hurt something of yours.

It's that latter issue coming back into play at my house. There's no diaper on a six-foot-six, three-hundred-pound, twenty-something that returns home for board and care. And anything else you might do to get your point across could be construed as assault and battery. No matter how much returning adult children frustrate you, and they will, you don't want to end up on a segment of *Cops*. Television adds ten-to-fifteen extra pounds to your figure and those fuzzy circles rarely hide your true identity.

Can you imagine your snob of a brother-in-law seeing the episode, and yelling, "Hey, Cheryl, isn't that your sister?"

"Where?"

"Right there next to the squad car."

"Oh, my gawd, you're right. I'd recognize those thighs anywhere. I've begged her to throw away those shorts."

The word detach, to be relevant for parents of Boomerang children, is a psychobabble term probably created in the wild Seventies while trying to maintain your sanity during adversity. When the rest of the world is competing in rigorous Olympic-game style to wrench sanity away from you, detach your emotions and hold on to your composure with both white-knuckled hands.

You remember sanity—that brief respite between surviving years of adolescent hormonal turbulence and the day they showed up again at the front door with belongings in hand. For me it lasted a whopping thirty seconds. One minute my husband and I were alone in the house, planning to redecorate, maybe enjoy a romantic vacation get away, and the next they were back. What did your Boomerangs tell you when they showed up at your door, asking to be let in? How did the sob story go? Was snow falling? Did you hear violins playing in the background? Do you remember somewhere in their conversation the word "temporary?" Temporary is a slippery concept. For you the word denotes a few months, for them it means a few years.

Sometimes I feel like the main character roles in *Hansel and Gretel* have been switched. Oh, the basics start out the same. I have two (grown) children in my house, and I'm the wicked witch, that part is obvious. However, I think they're waiting and watching for the opportunity to shove me into the oven and take over the candy-trimmed house.

Detachment is purely a mind game you have to practice, practice, practice. No additional expenses necessary, no equipment to assemble, no magic wand to wave in making it happen. Just you. Like learning to play the piano with your hands tied behind your back, though, it's going to take slow, deliberate baby steps and patience. Teach yourself to go far, far away in your mind, away from stress, away from them.

Detaching becomes a series of mantras you whisper to yourself over and over as the returning adult children begin to take over your house and your life while sucking the precious oxygen right out of your system because they can't manage to breathe on their own. They want yours.

Detach yourself. Sounds like it should be a top-40 Motown single by the Rondelles, doesn't it? Someone put a catchy tune to it, and we'll make it our theme song, please. How does detaching work, you desperately ask. Blow your nose, dry your tears, make sure the bathroom door is locked while you're reading this, and let me show you some examples.

When adult children gang up on you the second you walk in the door at night, detach. Take deep cleansings breaths. Inhale; tell yourself they can't get to you. Never make eye contact, they take it as a challenge. Exhale. This is your life; you are a successful human being. Inhale. You will watch the evening news and know there are worse situations in the world. Exhale.

Good—let's try another one. You wake up in the morning and find they left you a half a cup of sludge in the bottom of the pot, and sections of the newspaper scattered from bathroom to kitchen. Detach. Inhale. You will use the exercise of finding the newspaper to help get a great looking body. Exhale. Think positive thoughts. They were looking in the want ads for a job. Inhale. You want to make a fresh pot of coffee anyway—that thick stuff is from the cheap generic brand you leave in the cupboard. Exhale. At least they are up, dressed, and out of the house this morning. Inhale. Unlock your secret stash of fresh ground Starbucks you've stored in an old Tupperware container marked Brown Sugar and exhale. See, you're getting the idea.

When the noise level in the house, from multiple television sets blasting away and the grandchildren screeching at each other, becomes painful for the neighbor's dog two blocks down the road, run away. Don't hesitate; don't look back. Run. Some things even detaching exercises won't help.

When Boomerangs spend an entire day doing absolutely nothing then start asking you when dinner will be ready, think of wind swept beaches painted in glorious sunset colors at Cabo San Lucas or Maui—you know, all those faraway places you could never afford to visit while paying for braces and saving for college tuition. Use your imagination and sail away to a tropical paradise where gorgeous waiters bring you frosty tall glasses of boat drinks with little paper umbrellas and a slice of pineapple perched on the rim of the glass while you recline on a chase lounge. Soothing serenades of crashing waves and sea birds replace the blaring television.

After the twenty-something son manages to leave the back door open, in the dead of winter, for the third time in less than a month, and a puddle of rainwater collects by the doorway, think of swooshing down white powdered mountains on a crystal clear morning. You look fantastic, darling, in a gorgeous ensemble of matching skiwear and boots. Well, you would have learned how to ski if you hadn't paid for years of music lessons and countless pairs of tennis shoes.

Here's one of my favorite detachment exercises when the intensity of life threatens to crack my thin hold on composure. I think of winning thirty-two million dollars in the state lottery and leaving them out of my will. Brings a smile to my weary face every time.

Let me give you an example of cause and effect where detachment is a healthy alternative. When the son borrows my car, I can count on an empty gas tank, the driver's seat in a fully reclined position, and the radio cranked to a volume guaranteed to shatter my eardrums. During the three minutes it takes to make the car operable again, I choose to try to solve world peace. That's detachment. Practice—you'll find it beats swearing under your breath and getting your blood pressure all worked up. They don't care if you have a coronary. They're counting on it!

What's interesting is you can practice detachment and the little home-again darlings won't have a clue what you're doing. These twenty-something rejects of reality think of the word detach in computer-ese language, meaning to remove data files or some such techno-lingo bandied about by geeks everywhere today. (Praise Microsoft.) You want to skill yourself in the hard core, self-serving definition of the word, used to mentally get through a bad situation intact. They won't have a clue, I'm telling you. It's mah-va-lous.

"Bets, I swear my mother has Alzheimer's. The woman stares blankly over my shoulder when I'm talking to her. It's a good thing I'm home since divorcing Darrin. The woman obviously needs someone to keep an eye on her. Thank God she still knows how to make great meatloaf."

"Dang, girlfriend, it's contagious. My mom's the same way since I came home. I tried to tell her what a twit the CEO was, dumping us all after the merger with ViDex, totally blowing my portfolio, and she's humming. Totally oblivious to the conversation I'm having and my pain. Does menopause like short-circuit the brain?"

Which leads me to another definition of detaching according to the dictionary, which is to remove from association with something. Remove yourself. How big is your house? Trust me, it's never big enough when the kids move back home unless you're fortunate enough to own a multi-leveled mansion with separate wings. And if that's the case, you have enough money to pay them off to move to a new location. (It's called the Kept Kid Phenomenon and is a whole other book.)

I tried the poor man's escape route and moved out of state. Loaded everything we owned into a generic big red moving van and bought a new house in a two-acre forest over a thousand miles away. Sounds dreamy, doesn't it? My fantasy cottage for two ended up being a ranch-styled four bedroom, two and a half bath after continuous whining and finagling by the husband, which is a whole other Dr. Phil-we-need-to-talk issue. My romantic-second-half-of-life scenario lasted maybe an hour. Six people and countless pets now live here in over-crowded paradise.

How far can I remove myself when home is only an eighteen-hundred-square-foot house? I lock myself in the cramped master bedroom for a little peace and quiet. I pretend it's a hotel room and hole up with a stack of best sellers and a six-pack of Diet Coke. I don't recommend taking more than one of Oprah's former book club selections with you; the topics are usually dire and intense. You're already living the soap opera, *All My Grown Children*; you don't need to read more suffering and sorrow.

Seriously, it's more like I'm in a pre-World War II motel room since there's no room to turn around in my own bedroom. And I swear these walls are made out of tissue paper. What do contractors think when they throw tract houses up in two minutes with nothing in the walls for sound-proofing? It's all about the almighty profit dollars—build and sell people a house where kids can hear you unwrap a candy bar from three rooms away. Where is my insulation? Where's my padded cell?

Let me warn you, at least 90% of the time physically detaching yourself from home is not the answer. Being chased from your own home, even for brief respites, gives them the upper hand in using all your worldly possessions while you're gone. Stay tough. Giving them time to dig their lazy butt roots deeper into the frayed carpet is not the way to regain your ultimate freedom. I understand times come when you have to get out of the house or wind up on the ten o'clock news. All I'm saying is use moderation and good judgment. Adult children believe possession is nine-tenths of the law.

Here's an example of escaping within controlled boundaries. I do my weekly grocery shopping at five-thirty on Sunday morning, in baggy sweats and slippers. It's okay because A) I'm one of those perky morning people and the store is blissfully empty of most of the human race, and B) the adult children are sound asleep and less able to do damage while I'm gone. Also, I can annoy the heck out of my non-morning returnees around seven when I drag in the truckloads of groceries. Hey, get your jollies where you can. If they want to eat, they better at least help you bring in and put away the groceries—except the few bags of personal delicacies you've hidden under your arm, a sacred bag of junk food for yourself, like a bag of Hershey's Kisses. These go in your secret stash. More on that later in another chapter.

The palace of Wal-Mart, open 24/7, is an excellent entertainment escape of choice, if you can keep from buying out the place to relieve your frustrations. Try a new lipstick color or a new pair of shoes. Listen to a few CD selections or read the entire collection of Shoebox cards from Hallmark. You can enter big W any hour of the day or night, wandering up and down the aisles, and at least three friendly faces say hi to you. Okay, they're paid to be nice to you, but take a smiling human being whenever you can get it. Most Wal-Mart's have a McDonald's or soda fountain inside where you get unlimited Diet Coke refills to stay hydrated during your search for solitude.

After a few months of ditching your kids (I mean detaching yourself), you may run out of economical places to hide. The local librarian may kick you out due to government budget cuts closing their doors early, but while you can, settle in the peace and quiet and read the local newspaper or two. Check out all the quality periodicals you can't afford now with kids back in the house. Use the local shopping malls strictly for exercising, a free mini workout (warning, leave your credit cards at home—locked away.) You don't want to hang around too long or the security guard will start posting your photo as a known vagrant.

When the concept of detaching your mind and emotions doesn't work for you any more, and it will happen, it's time to look up the word in the dictionary again. To reiterate, the more classic definitions state to separate or unfasten. Difficult times call for drastic measures. When detaching your emotions doesn't work, detachment of the phone and the television will help. Be creative. This is not the Martha Stewart relationship hour; you need survival tactics. Start detaching things. Unplug, unfasten, let go. They're your plugs; you have the power.

Being pushed over the proverbial cliff is when the large, overgrown toddler uses your phone for the three millionth time in one day. When my daughter was a teen-ager (long ago and far away) I found it a wise investment giving her a separate phone line for her bedroom. The few extra dollars a month insured the main phone number into the house rang only for us grown-ups. Or I could dial out any time without begging permission from some adolescent locked in the closet with the phone cord stretched across the floor. When she left home (the first time), the second phone line became our data line for the computer's modem. A simple technical transition and easy to do. How foolish we were letting our guard down.

When Boomerangs return, what's the first thing they latch onto? Okay, after raiding the kitchen for a full-course meal and a gallon of the name-brand soda you started buying once they moved out. The phone. They have to let half the population of the United States under thirty know what their new phone number will be and catch up on the latest gossip since their last conversation. When was that, a few hours ago? Suddenly the phone is ringing every twenty minutes. Grand Central Station, may I help you?

You become an unpaid answering service again. Don't you remember this irritating job description tacked onto your resume during their teen-age years? God help you if you forget to write one down for the Boomerang; remember, this personal service is never a two-way street. Oh, the IRS called last week? Something about penalties? But you couldn't write it down because your nails were drying?

Is there a federal or state law that says you have to have a telephone in the house? Of course not. Generations of people have lived and do live their lives without the constant harassment of telephone solicitors. Hard to believe, but it's true. How those poor people got through a night's dinner without being badgered for aluminum siding or a new long distance carrier is beyond comprehension.

I say cancel your in-home telephone service altogether. Unplug the equipment and invest in a cellular phone just for you and your husband or if you're a single mom, a cell phone just for you. Enjoy the peace and quiet of no solicitors by using the cell phone as your choice for communication with the outside world. A lot of you already have one or two. If the Boomerang whiners ask to use the phone, tell them there's a pay phone down the street. Or maybe it's time they get their own apartment, hint, hint.

Are the holidays or their birthdays around the corner? Go shopping at your local Wal-Mart or Costco and pick them up a multi-minutes phone card. You can get them a pre-paid phone card (rates are anywhere from four to six cents a minute) they can use at any friend's house or pay phone. The cards come in a variety of colorful styles depending on the communication carrier and in increments of 30, 60 or more minute durations. Telephone calls are privileges, not a guaranteed right when they move back home. This is not cruel and unusual punishment no matter what they tell you; trust me. Do not make them comfortable; they will never leave.

What about television? You don't want them growing spoiled and sprouting as couch potatoes planted in front of the tube for hours and hours. I admit once upon a time the TV and I had a great parental relationship while raising children together. An hour of *Sesame Street* in the morning before work meant I could plunk Junior on his butt in front of a singing Big Bird and fold the weekly heaps of clean laundry in a non-combative way. Ever tried wrestling clean underwear from a toddler who just finished eating an Oreo cookie? It's not pretty.

Later years of television in our house proved helpful as the pre-adolescent munchkins watched inane hours of prime time originals (currently rerunning on Nick at Nite) once they'd finished their homework. Okay, more like an electronic babysitter to keep them from killing each other during those last desperate hours before bedtime. (Twenty-plus years ago parents weren't faced with MTV and PG-13 rating systems.) The well-paid censors of the Sixties and early Seventies (supported by grateful grandparents everywhere) made sure the nighttime situation comedy shows were pure mind-numbing saccharine.

To watch television during the 21st century, you practically have to own a satellite dish or subscribe to a local cable company. Most neighborhoods outlaw any form of TV antennas on top of houses, for aesthetic reasons the covenants claim. More likely insurance companies created this ruling, tired of paying off medical claims for men who slipped off icy roofs trying to adjust the antennas during Super Bowl.

Want to limit the grown kiddies from living in your house until eternity? Disconnect the television. Get reacquainted with your spouse and use the money saved from cable payments for monthly massages. You deserve them. If you can't imagine living without television yourself, order basic cable only. Enough stations to broadcast you the world news and education channels, with maybe a few stations that show the ancient black and white movies thrown in for entertainment. Boomerangs hate the lack of color. Remember, every movie channel you subscribe to gives them that much more reason not to move out of Mom's house.

Have your girlfriend tape the *Sex in the City* shows for you and watch them when the kids are out. You can use the VCR with a television that is not connected to cable service. Invest in an annual Blockbuster rental card and ask the clerks to keep it hidden behind the counter under an assumed name. Be adventurous—make a date with your spouse and take him to an actual movie theater once in a while. When was the last time you two shared a bucket of popcorn together? Do not include the Boomerangs during these outings. A taste of free entertainment only makes them want more.

If you must have cable television in the house, and I can't stress enough to make sure it is only basic cable channels, do not allow cable access in their bedrooms. Don't fall for their piecrust promises of paying you each month for the additional outlets. (Remember Mary Poppins? The spoonful of sugar lady? Easily made, easily broken was her definition of piecrust promises.) Unless you're prepared to have them under your roof until h-e-double-hockey-sticks freezes over, do *not* give them private cable access. Don't make me call the sanity police on you!

Then there's the desktop computer, the latest electronic family household appliance—the metal treasure chest of fun and information you thought belonged to you once the kids moved out. Maybe you went shopping at Costco or Gateway for the latest and greatest in gigabyte heaven once the fledglings moved out the first time. You now had available computer time for looking up instant gourmet recipes and finally writing that great American novel you've had floating around in your head since you were seven years old. When adult children come home they gravitate to the machine like metal to a magnet. You go to answer your email and find a twenty-something child hunched over the keyboard with a layer of dust on their head and shoulders because they haven't moved in three days. I hate when that happens.

Even before my Boomerangs came home it was impossible to log on in the evenings, because hubby spent hours with his own daily agenda on the Internet, finding car parts we don't need, fishing boats I threatened to kill him with if one found its way home, and obscure purchases on eBay.com.

In a perfect world, our weekends would start at nine a.m. with the garage sales from the classified section of our local newspaper circled and mapped out plus a fannie pack filled with single dollars and quarters. Pouring over someone else's cast offs is intoxicating. The challenge of finding a treasure among the trash brings the thrill of victory to an experienced saler like my husband.

Or we drive down a busy street on a sunny Saturday morning with one objective in mind like getting a new garbage disposal and the lure of colored signs and hand drawn arrows staked into the ground or taped to road signs beckons him unmercifully. We end up taking twisted turns on a dozen different side streets searching for the Holy Grail of yard sales. Two hours later, a seven-mile excursion has turned into a thirty-three mile adventure ride.

For a garage sale junkie like my husband, eBay.com is like going into a diabetic coma from gorging on chocolate. Whoever created this virtual auction and bargain network connecting almost fifty million registered users in the world's largest yard sale deserves a Nobel peace prize for uniting people in shopping sprees everywhere.

Husbands and significant others take note—to score major points with the other half take yourself to eBay.com land. Granted most of the time my guy is getting himself into hot water bidding on hundreds of dollars worth of gadgets only another person with strong testosterone would appreciate. Thank goodness some fool usually out bids him in the last hours. However, my Christmas presents from him have become very personal and eclectic since he's been shopping online.

An incredible thing happened one year, hubby realized by typing in my favorite things (sounds like a great line for a song) the value of his gift selections for me went off the Richter scale. EBay.com made shopping a month or so before any big day simple, yet a delightful challenge, and the man loves a good challenge.

Let me show you an easy example of this phenomenon. His fav singer is Jimmy Buffett. Buffett is a mega corporation that sends us gift catalogs of parrot head apparel, trinkets, and fun I can peruse at leisure and order items for holidays and anniversaries. One of my favorites, however, is Harry Chapin (*Cats in the Cradle*), a legend who left the earth due to a horrible car accident in the early Eighties, leaving only a dozen albums and stories to remember him by.

Imagine my surprise to find hubby had amassed for me a perfect CD collection of Chapin's music. The wickedly talented president of the Kathleen Shaputis fan club worked with hubby and created a unique decorated box set I will treasure forever. Run, don't walk to eBay.com and type in spouse's favorite things and you'll find a wealth of birthday, anniversary and holiday gifts sure to be the popular topic of conversations.

If your husband can't get to the computer because of Boomerangs leeching themselves to the Internet, none of this magic will happen. Bump those puppies off the keyboard. The possibilities of heavenly gift-wrapped surprises depend on your significant other having access to the keyboard.

Even my grandchildren rush in from elementary and preschool, give a quick kiss hi, and head for the computer to play games in my dining-room-converted-office. I don't stand a chance of using my own equipment, unfortunately, with two of them living with me. The preschooler has to sit on my lap to play. At his age he wants an audience, and someone to click on replay. When he was two and a half years old his first cognitive paragraph was "Play Power Rangers on 'puter. He jump. He fall in hole." I'm surprised our dogs haven't learned how to use the computer to check out Lassie.com or order pounds of spicy dog biscuits online.

What's a woman to do? Get serious; defend your computer rights. If you're the generous Donna Reed kind of mom, make up a schedule and everyone is assigned specific computer times. As I've said before about the telephone, the computer is a privilege not a guaranteed right. Especially for adult children. The local library has Internet access, make them check their email there.

To cut them off your system cold turkey, remove the plug. If you're using a modem to access the Internet, detach the phone cord and keep it locked in a drawer. Or remove the power cord to keep them off the machine completely. No cord, no Internet. Don't try hiding it in your purse. Your husband might be afraid to journey into the faux leather pouch of no return, but your kids are probably experienced in digging around for loose money. If you have cable access to the Internet, because you took my advice and kept in-home phone service out of the house, you hide the network cord. It's a little more bulky, but worth the hassle if you want them off your computer.

If you can't bring yourself to block them from using the computer (we'll work on this over the course of the book), be strong about using passwords. Most of your favorite Web sites will ask for user identification and a password. When you check in, you get a digital salutation, like your own Wal-Mart greeter. As a former computer technician, let me give you a few password tips. Remember you're dealing with mentalities that grew up with passwords, and I don't mean the popular television game show hosted by Alan Ludden. It's amazing how their twenty-something-year-old fingers can't operate a vacuum cleaner or balance their checkbook, yet they fly over a keyboard with mind boggling dexterity.

Don't use your children or grandchildren's first names, the dog's name, or your wedding anniversary as a password. Don't panic, there are lots of choices left. Use something simple, like the word MINE. Or ALLMINE. You can't use spaces in a password; multiple words have to be lumped together. Passwords are usually limited to four to eight characters, whether you use numbers, letters, or both.

Using THESEKIDSAREDRIVINGMECRAZY won't work, sorry.

I've thought of something else you can detach. Remember how I said it takes three minutes to readjust everything in my car once the big kid has driven it? Well, the frustration is similar when my daughter drives it. Except the seat is under the steering wheel and she has all the windows rolled down. Have someone show you how to detach the distributor cap on the car or have the local mechanic install a hidden kill switch under the dash. Have you noticed the Boomerangs tell you they'll be back in an hour as they grab the car keys, but you don't see them for two days? Or a quick run to the drug store for Nyquil because they supposedly have a cold means the car won't be back until two in the morning. Your first clue they weren't really sick was when they didn't ask you to go out and get them the medicine.

Most Boomerang kids come back to the parental nest with some sort of mechanical transportation to clog up your driveway, but using their own car would mean filling it with gas and checking the oil once in a while. Or it's in a constant state of disrepair, so they grab your keys. Try using your own car for any length of time and be amazed at the guilt trip they try to lay on you. Potential job interviews are missed because you had the nerve to use the car for something pathetic like having a root canal without checking with them. You know their lives are more important than yours. Not!

Here's a handy-dandy solution. Make arrangements to park in front of your neighbor's yard on the next block. When the kids ask you what happened to the car, tell them it's at the shop. When you leave the house the next day, pretend you're carpooling or taking the bus. It's a win/win situation—you get exercise walking around the block and use of your own car.

Keep breathing and remain calm. Since you can't detach the kids, detach yourself; then detach the services in your home. Sacrificing a little convenience today will save you hours of expensive therapy in the long run. If not on the psychologist's couch, definitely on the masseuse's table. My adult kids can erase the rubbery relaxed feeling of a great one-hour massage in less than three seconds flat. I know. I might as well throw massage money out the car window. It would last longer and maybe make someone else happy.

2

Who Left the Door Unlocked?

Safety proofing your home is what they call it when you cover, lock, and shield everything in sight because you have toddlers in the house. Once the darlings are up and mobile, you must protect them from their own rabid curiosity and ambition. Infants asleep in a crib or dribbling all over your shoulder are adorable, lulling you into a false sense of security. Once they learn to walk they are capable of mass destruction. Running loose on their own, a toddler becomes a terrifying moving object with multiple appendages that grab, throw, and rearrange objects and whole rooms faster than Martha Stewart on a bad day.

As the parent of a short one you become creative in dealing with movable objects. In my initial mommy years I held down toilet lids from prying fingers with a three-pound unabridged version of Webster's Dictionary so I wasn't explaining to the plumber why I needed a third service call in less than a month for removing house keys or other important items from the trap. These days I'm sure a few toddlerettes have tossed a remote control or two into the bowl to see if Daddy's favorite toy floats. Trust me, they don't. It's not a pretty sight. At Target or Wal-Mart you can buy any number of baby safety products such as plastic covers to fit over electrical outlets and keep tiny fingers from digging into the dark slats with shiny pennies to see what's in there.

Maybe you were the safety consciousness parent in your neighborhood people talked about as a great example, having not only a home filled with love and comfort, but a safe house as well. I'll bet you were an over-achiever in high school, too, probably first on your block with expensive security gates on the stairs and a baby monitor receiver in every room. Back in the Sixties and Seventies, we didn't have catalogs filled with pages of make-life-easier gadgets for infants and how-did-a-parent-ever-live-without do-hickeys for toddlers. We pretty much kept our miniature descendants confined in a three by three playpen when we tired from carrying them on our hip or chasing them after they went into mobilization.

Toddlers need protection, we all agree. From talk show hosts doing storylines on tips to prevent child abduction to Big Bird and Elmo on *Sesame Street* teaching fire safety, everyone tries to help. Short people under five years old do not have a mature understanding of cause-and-effect physics and natural consequences. They depend on us, as parents, to keep them safe.

Adult children who return home are like tall toddlers, and I want to talk about adult-child proofing your home. The end result may seem strange, but the logical concept is the same as when they were cute and cuddly. You're protecting their health by protecting your house. The less they abuse your stuff, the more likely you are not to hurt them. The abuse to your home this time around won't be peanut butter and jelly sandwiches shoved into the VCR. Think Chinese water torture with each drop being the irritation of someone else using your things, and annoying your life. Empty toilet paper rolls will take on gigantic proportions.

Starting from the moment they move back into the nest, the added bodies, noise and clutter take on larger-than-life proportions. Someone else using all the hot water throws off your schedule, you can't pull your car out of the driveway because theirs blocks it. The teensy details of another person invading your home when you thought you'd finished parenting are killers—details such as another radio blaring from their room or the bathroom or an additional television creating another layer of noise. Extra wet coats piled in the entryway on a rainy evening might be just more than you can handle after sitting on a freeway backed up for miles and no dinner started. Or worse yet, finally getting in the door and stepping on something soft and pungent because your adult son didn't remember to walk his dog.

After eighteen or twenty-some years of raising your children to be independent adults, the reward is a quiet house where all is right with the world. The freedom to put out a shell shaped dish of fragrant guest soaps in the hall bathroom and know that only guests will use them.

Returning adult children, especially those bringing offspring with them, add a maniacal energy to the mix of life that is not always easy to take. And it's not like you can run off and join the Foreign Legion at this stage of your life either. You're no flipping ingénue, there's no place to hide. Who left the door unlocked? Who let all these people into the house?

Where better to start your attack and take back what is rightfully yours than in the kitchen? This is not a 24-hour diner; they can't get everything their way three meals a day, plus snacks. It's not an all-you-can-eat buffet, either. They don't understand your frustration, they think it's Mom's kitchen, she loves me, and she'll feed me.

Raise your hand if you've walked into the kitchen with your mouth watering for a taste of something sweet for dessert to find out someone had snuck in before you and cleaned the shelves bare? I hate when that happens. You endured it when the children were under age and the laws of the state stipulated you will provide nourishment and shelter until they are of legal age. But once they stand a foot taller than you and can enjoy gambling at the bottom floor of Circus Circus in Las Vegas without being thrown out as underage, some of the laws revert to your side.

You have the right to eat your own leftovers. I enjoy cold pizza for breakfast or eating cold chow mein from the carton the next day. I'll buy bigger portions of something from a restaurant for the simple pleasure of early morning leftovers. Not with Boomerangs in the house. If a fast food container or a doggie bag makes it into the refrigerator, a twenty-something-year-old vacuum inhales the contents in the middle of the night.

Did you know there's not a law on the books says you have to leave the refrigerator in your house available during business hours to people over the age of twenty-one? I've looked. It's true. If a Boomerang ever gets into public office I'm sure this loophole won't last, but for now you're legally covered.

Imagine my post-parental horror of seeing two hundred dollars worth of groceries disappear minutes after entering the house. Before I've finished bringing everything in from the car, the sacks are pitifully limp and empty on the floor and counter tops. I say if you go shopping at the local Safeway grocery store and bring home sacks of delicious entrées and ingredients of joy, you do not have to share them with any member of the family you gave birth to older than two decades. Post a sign in the kitchen they must forage for themselves outside of your home.

Granted their doe-eyed look of suffering and confusion will catch you off guard. And the pouting and whining can be a real nuisance when company comes over on the weekends. Remember when all you prayed about were the kids behaving when the boss came over for dinner? Those were innocent days. You're not trying to impress management for a raise any more; most of us are on the downhill run towards retirement. It's embarrassing when food disappears just before company arrives, leaving you with only a limp carrot stick and two soggy pickles for appetizers. Makes for a long evening while you call for take-out.

Stay firm, girlfriend. If these overgrown relations have been harboring themselves in your home for longer than a few months, toughen up, get serious, and lock the main chamber of nourishment—the refrigerator.

How, you may ask? I have just the thing—the handy-dandy Post-Parental Privacy Lock. This new and improved invention for CNS sufferers has a clear plastic two-part base that's almost invisible. Self-stick tape adheres one part on either side of the refrigerator door. Flip the clear plastic latch down and hook your ultra-chic mini-combination padlock, from a rainbow of decorator colors, through the hole and, ta-da, you're all set. It sits near the top of the appliance, nothing gaudy, nestled in among a couple of colorful magnets. Your company and relatives won't even know its there. Install a PPP lock today on your refrigerator and sleep tonight knowing your Mrs. What's-her-name's cinnamon bun will be there in the morning. Right where you left it. For peace of mind in protecting a piece of cheesecake, I'm telling you it's heaven.

No ordinary padlocks are these of blah brass and tarnish found at the local hardware store by the guy who hasn't changed his t-shirt since Reagan was in office. You may choose from a variety of luscious colors, sizes, and styles for every kitchen design. Functional and color-coordinated, what could be better to preserve your frozen food items and icy Diet Cokes from marauding Boomerangs? If you've created a Better Homes and Garden cooking haven in colonial blues and white, there's a slate tone just for you. If you've decorated your chef domain in perky yellows and reds, pick a primary color padlock to ensure your peace of mind. Or let the lock blend in with the color of the appliance and use white, almond, or aluminum. God help us if they go back to making our appliances avocado green and golden rod. We'll adapt locks to earth tones, but only if needed.

Just when I thought I could down size the double door behemoth I needed when my kids were growing up for something cute and compact from Sears with an ice maker and distilled water in the door, here comes a parade of twenty-something's with their colorful floats of little people into my house and kitchen. With this many people living here a sub-zero walk-in unit isn't big enough to hold the weekly grocery purchases.

If the refrigerator carries the title of being one of the most important appliances in the kitchen, I doubt you'll need a PPP lock for the dishwasher. No threat comes to this major appliance as they haven't invented one that loads and unloads itself yet, and until that day it will always be the abandoned nobody-loves-me-everybody-hates-me piece.

I've seen my adult children return home and start taking out a clean plate for each individual serving of a meal, one for salad, one for the main course, and another for dessert. Funny, I didn't see one of those restaurant plate dispensers with a huge spring at the bottom installed, but obviously they thought they did. With each new plate of food went a separate utensil. Excuse me, you lick the fork clean between courses, one fork does all. When they had to do the dishes, one fork could have lasted a week. Now one meal for one adult child takes a full set of Corningware, Oneida, and a few yards of paper towels.

Recently I had to replace my dishwasher, though, after another generation of sipper cups caked with dried milk and stacks of sticky cereal bowls filled the upper racks. Poor thing, couldn't remove leftover Spaghetti-O's any more. The daily loads were too much for her.

Ranking a close number two in the kitchen appliance race for our hearts is the microwave. Did you know today's college students were born after the invention of the microwave? They've probably never seen popcorn made on the stove in a pan with oil, and would shudder to think a hot dog had to be boiled in water to be cooked, unless paying top dollar for one to a New York City street vendor.

My grudge isn't against my adult kids using the microwave. The whole point of the appliance is fast food and the ability to get you in and out of the kitchen quickly. That's a good thing. Store shelves are filled with ready to heat containers of every known food group. Even soup comes ready to eat with a quick ride in the 'Wave. Doesn't take long to heat up a burrito or nuke a frozen entrée, as any twenty-something knows.

What bothers me is the explosions of splattered spaghetti on all four walls and sauce drips on the ceiling they leave behind that forced me to add a PPP lock to the microwave. That and the fact the grandchildren started cooking for themselves. Once a frozen snack went into my microwave by an overly independent short person. Hitting three minutes, instead of thirty seconds, the young lad melted the object into a block of cement. I picked a darling black satin three-number combo lock to dangle just under the handle.

Want to know what irritates me quicker than dog hair in my cream cheese? One of the adult kids leaving laundry in the washer or dryer during the weekend. The boss at my day-job gives me two days a week to stay home and catch up on my personal chores, such as housework and laundry. When my arms are filled with dirty clothes ready to throw in my Kenmore washer and I find someone's wet duds wadded in the bottom of the tub, I can't tell you what runs through my mind because this is a PG-rated book; you don't want the grisly four-letter-word details. Or opening the dryer and finding it overstuffed with baggy clothes from days ago.

I hate having to ask or wait my turn to use my own washer and dryer. I give the Boomerangs Monday through Friday, five days out of the week to my measly two, that's the majority, more than fair to get their rinse and dry fluffed and folded. Can they remember? No. Hello, I work for a living and have earned the privilege of in-home appliances.

I collected my Girl Scout badge of domestic honor as a newlywed and later as a new mother. After years of schlepping plastic laundry baskets piled high every week to the downtown laundromat in stained clothing I found on the floor of my closet, I refuse to ever again sit under those awful florescent lights, in muggy temperatures, with three hundred machines humming.

Out come two handy-dandy Post-Parental Privacy Locks—one for the washer and one for the dryer. I leave the appliances unlocked during the workweek. Come Friday night I clean out the two machines and lock 'em down. Such a tiny step for me and a giant leap for sanity as I ease into my weekend.

I've heard other parents suggest installing coin-operated machines into the laundry room. I'm sorry; I don't see it because the second time they asked for change from a dollar, the very same dollar they borrowed from me the night before, I'd have to hurt something. This is a migraine headache waiting to happen. If they don't have the money to move out, where's the money for clean laundry going to come from? Stay alert from false prophets of quick fix solutions. The sooner the Boomerangs are out on their own, the sooner you have your house back. Trust me. The PPP locks will give you a chance to breathe easier while waiting for them to move out.

Bill Cosby said, "I brought you into this world, and I can take you out again." If adult children keep using and abusing your kitchen appliances and washroom equipment the way mine do, you have the right to threaten to send them back where they came from. Literally. My man, Cos. The line doesn't scare mine any more, but maybe yours are still impressionable.

I've got someone new to add to your Christmas list. Make the guy that runs the self-storage place on the other side of town your new best friend. Have you wondered why those cinder-block mini-malls of locked closets are cropping up everywhere? It's because when Boomerangs move back, you have to rent one to hold all the furniture they've collected in the short time since they left home.

I'm talking a long-term relationship with this guy. Bring him a case of Miller beer and a big smile. You are going to need him longer than you expect. He will become part of the family as he watches you trudge in and out with loads of familial junk.

With a revolving door of who moves in and out of our house, we have a storage unit with our name engraved on a plaque by the door. You'll find with a crowded nest it is not just adult children returning, it can be your aging parents moving in, joining the flock. You end up storing their antiques and boxes of fifty years worth of accumulated stuff. Pieces of household items you grew up with, the familiar kitchen ware, the floor lamp you nestled under watching late night black and white television. Let's not forget boxes of *Condensed Readers Digest Books*.

Or the grandchildren move in and you're carting high chairs and cribs in and out of the storage unit as one grows up and another baby comes in. You know the baby rule—don't sell that stuff off, because as soon as you think no more grandkids, here comes another one.

Keep the storage office number on speed dial. Treat the staff kindly, and they'll let you in after hours on those emergency runs where you need something important stored in the box on the bottom of the first row. It happens.

Some day I want to store my own memorable, valuable stuff in the storage unit and live in a house free of clutter and care. I've paid years of rental for everyone else. It'd be like dumping my thirty-pound purse into an oversized Rubbermaid container so I can walk around with a black velvet cocktail napkin on a chain.

Like that's ever going to happen. My purse is an extension of my life. Divided sections include medicinal relief of sinus tablets and antacids, three hundred identification cards from Barnes & Noble's discount card to Petco. Pocket sized wipes, sealed packets of Shout for those invariable stains at a restaurant, snacks, loose change, and a variety of pens. I could probably exist out of it for quite a while if I find myself in one of those *Reader Digest's Real Life Drama's* where my car skids off an embankment and no one finds me for days. People in the family expect me to have things on hand, a genetic problem passed on to me from my mother—the original fifty-pound purse woman.

But I digress; let's continue our journey of adult-child proofing the house with the main bathroom, the one in the center hallway meant for family and guests if we had some. I make it a habit not to invite anyone over, under any circumstances, any time. The less of the world's population exposed to my organized chaos, the better. You can all stop taking personally why the famous author wouldn't invite you to dinner at her abode. Or why I threw myself bodily against the door blocking you from coming inside for a simple cup of tea. It's best to meet me at a restaurant.

Short grandchildren and two adult children make up the majority of daily users for this bathroom. Six-foot-six guy has to share a shower with a plastic basket filled with action figures and cartoon characters while spongy red, blue, and green alphabet letters decorate the sides of the tub. You'd think that alone would hasten his departure for a bathroom of his own. No, a free shower is a free shower no matter who or what you share it with.

Here's a handy dandy item to add to your home security arsenal—a toilet lock. A cute plastic designer toilet lock keeps toddlers from falling head first into the water or throwing their toys into the bowl and flushing hard pieces of plastic into the system. What a great concept to use against the adult child who's not getting the message of worn out welcome. Bottom (no pun intended) line is when push comes to shove, lock the john and see how long before the kids get the hint and move out. They'll tire of driving to the gas station/mini mart down the street to use the bathroom. When the clerk sees them night after night, maybe he'll suggest getting a place of their own.

No tools required for this jim-dandy gadget, either. The plastic unit slips into place over the lid and under the rim, for fairly easy release. Remember, since it was made to keep a toddler out, and easy access for the parent, you want to add a Post-Parenting Privacy combination padlock, and you're set to keep Big John out of the porcelain john.

Does their aim into the bowl get any better with age? We excused them when their stubby extension barely reached over the top of the rim. Then in middle school they were too hormonally challenged to keep it aimed in one direction too long. Is it impossible for an adult male to get everything into the toilet? Does a thirty-second attention span mean I have to clean up dribbles forever?

Continuing on the tour of the bathroom, check out the latest MediSafe locking device for the medicine cabinet. I hate to go into the bathroom with a pounding sinus headache for pain relief tablets and someone's emptied the bottle ahead of me. Bad enough with illegal drug labs making the news every five minutes, it takes an act of Congress for Joe Model Citizen to buy a bottle of Sudafed. You have to leave your finger-prints and life history before the pharmacy sells you a bottle. Too bad they never ask for the first-born child in payment. Where's Rumpelstiltskin when you need him?

The medicine safe denies little kids access to dangerous medications, and the older ones too, with a keypad combination lock or key. If a bad code is entered, or if the safe is left open for more than ten minutes, an alarm sounds. You want to keep your good stuff in here.

Use one of the Post-Parental Privacy locks for the bottom bathroom cabinets. Secure the storage of your extra deodorant and toothpaste; it's a major ravaging spot for Boomerangs. Personal hygiene products are the most expensive items on a grocery list and these buttheads are not stupid; they've been in the real world and know the price of Crest and Colgate even on sale at Target. Hide and lock the gold.

Including the toilet paper. Don't get me started on the topic of toilet paper. How can a man go through half a roll in one sitting? Add multiple people of the same oversized gender in the house, and I end up replacing a roll a day in each bathroom. We're going to have the Department of Ecol-ogy and Save Our Forests people picketing the house any day now. On the weekends store clerks turn my name in to the police for possible tee-peeing parties. They can't believe one family goes through that much toilet paper. I should get a direct link from the Charmin factory to our toilet.

I'm the type of person that when Target has their dollar sale or we get a refund on our income tax, I stock up on the personal necessity products in bulk. I buy bars of soap by the case. Shampoo comes in gallon jugs. It's okay; they're safely locked away with a couple of handy dandy PPP locks on the bathroom cabinets. Control, though, only lasts while it's in the cabinet.

Again, choose a PPP combination lock to match the décor. My main bathroom is done in a soft blue and burgundy. I can go either way on the color scheme of the locks in the bathroom having two strong colors in the design. I tend to go with blue, as a personal choice. I've matching towels. A treasured pen and ink drawing of the Balboa Island Fun Zone hangs on the wall, a watercolor with various blues. Husband and I shared many a memory there in our "courting" days. We even brought our kids along on a vacation or two. Little did we know sharing those days with them meant fewer of ever being without them.

Will husband notice if you add a lock to your bathroom cabinets? Probably not, and you ensure your own supplies aren't kidnapped while you're out of the house. If hubby runs out of soap or shampoo, he'll yell out the door at the exact moment you're busy doing something else. Same old, same old. Responsibility of replenishing stock items in the bathroom is the woman's job, he says; discussions of living with a mere male will be provided in a future book.

Does the hall linen closet need a lock? Maybe, maybe not. You want them to change their sheets now and again or get a fresh towel. I'll leave this one up to your discretion.

Inside the house you will find and create as many locked areas as needed. However, another area exists that adult children are inclined to raid as well, and that's the garage. The word borrowing rolls off an adult child's tongue like promises from a sleazy used car dealer wearing a tie with last week's gravy stains on it. The drawers of tools are like rows of candy to the adult son as his car and his life depend on using the conveniences held within the hallowed walls of his parent's garage.

Every cough or ping in their car needs something from hubby's world to tweak or fix it. Please, it's like listening to an old bear growling if any of those tools are misplaced and left lying about which frequently happens. I don't need to referee the event when confrontations happen.

Respect for the post-parental's things is usually the lacking component.

On one hand, tools were meant for using; on the other, leaving them out in the rain, or on the edge of the tool bench where they fall if someone slams a door, is enough to cause World War III in our neighborhood. The Sears Craftsman Department would sob at the mess the RAC's have left behind some days.

Part of the problem is they think their lives should continue in the manner they were accustomed. After living too long with Mom and Dad, they are incapable of living out in the real world without the conveniences they can't afford yet. Drills, bits, and handy-dandy tool belts are toys and delights to any twenty-something with a y in his chromosome. Though bonding time inside the room is memorable between father and son, unsupervised borrowing can be fatalistic. I'd suggest major padlocks, 8 digit combination locks, and let the spouse go crazy for a time at Home Depot. It's worth the peace of mind and sanity later. Lock up the extra cans of oil, the extra set of snow chains, whatever is important in the world of garages and cars.

Most of you have a tool shed on the property, which is not usually a problem with Boomerangs. Inside a tool shed you'd find lawn mowers, shovels, rakes, all the utensils you need as a homeowner, but equate to back breaking labor to a Boomerang. Locks are optional here. A rare returning adult child indulges in lawn care in payment for room and board. Maybe leaving a trail of Reese's peanut butter cups to the tool shed might entice them to try weeding the flower beds or sweeping the driveway, but they are not as innocent as ET. A trail of twenty-dollar bills would catch their attention, but at that price I'd hire a professional gardener and save the grief of listening to their moaning before and after anything happens in the yard.

When we bought the larger acreage in the Pacific Northwest, the first have-to-have toy was a John Deere rider mower. You'd think the Boomerang would enjoy doing something more fun than pushing a mower by hand. The novelty lasted one ride around the property for both hubby and son. All the whining and drooling over getting one dampened as soon as it moved into its own covered space by the tool shed. It's a necessary appliance, but new toys wear thin once they've been bought.

The eight-year-old grandson would sell his soul to be able to mow the lawn solo on a weekly basis. He sits with hubby most times and has steered in wide-open areas. You know as soon as he's old enough to drive the machine without crashing it into the house or the pine trees in the backyard, he will conveniently disappear on weekends for sports, Scouts, or hanging out with friends.

Knowing how we all suffer from our own little senior moments, I'll do a quick rerun of what we've just covered. This chapter shows you how to lock up your major appliances, including the microwave, with handy-dandy Post-Parental Privacy Padlocks. That's right, there's no law saying your home comes with free microwave services.

The locks blend in with any decor and are extremely functional. You and junior have great communication skills and don't think you need them? Just try to enjoy the luscious piece of New York Cheesecake topped with fresh strawberries you brought back from the restaurant last night. Boomerangs stare at you blank faced with "I didn't do it" on their lips, and cheesecake on their breath, as you scream pointing at the vacant spot where you know you left the container.

Parental Privacy Padlocks, the author's invention, are your new friends. Use lots and lots, all kinds and sizes, of these colored combination locks, with 10,000 possible codes, to match your interior designs in any kitchen or bathroom. If you chose to use regular padlocks when protecting your toothpaste and toilet paper from raiding adult children, keep the set of keys close to you at all times. You can lock drawers and cupboards to safe guard anything from extra batteries to clean towels.

3

Power Struggles
and Hot Flashes

If you find yourself caught between acting like an invited guest on the Oprah show in your own home, and Jerry Springer's guest, wanting to grab the nearest chair and duke it out with your child, you're in a power struggle. Compassion and frustration, two main ingredients when dealing with adult children, mix about as well as Balsamic vinegar and ice cream.

Turning red in the cheeks when the temperature is down below sixty is a hot flash. Seeing red and arguing in parent mode when the adult children do something irritating is a power struggle. Try not to mix the two up. Or take advantage of the hot flashes and get a few extra screams out of your system. They won't know the difference, and you'll feel better.

Menopausal mothers of returning adult children are to be sheltered and protected. Hormones are registering in the red zone and the slightest movement of any kind could send them ballistic. Think of padding a hydrogen bomb, you want this woman stabilized as much as possible, any time, all the time.

These post-hormonal women group together at lunch tables and café rooms everywhere in America, turning their attention to the screwed-up lives of their grown-up children. Releasing the pressure valve in the company of your peers is the greatest temporary solution. Pseudo counseling, in the form of whining and griping among them for an hour or more, gives back a thread of hope where darkness preyed before. Like an Oprah show in a day full of CNN headlines.

Whether you're working full-time or part-time, or tortured at home, make time with your girlfriends. Schedule lunch often and get out there, you need this. The open arms of a fellow sufferer are best, but even the shoulder of another mom will definitely band-aid the owie of dealing with Boomerang buttheads. They know, they care, and they're there for you.

Yelling "I'm the parent; you're the child" at a six-foot-six-inch twenty-something doesn't work, trust me. Trying to shout at someone when you have to climb a ladder to get his attention is very ineffective. They figure out what you're up to and disappear as soon as they hear you clunking the ladder out of the garage.

You can't put an adult child twice as big as you into time out either. Try sticking a three-hundred-pound adult into the corner with his nose against the wall. They don't fit. It didn't work all that well when he was eight years old. He's always been big for his age, now it's impossible.

Calling him a few choice names is more embarrassing than effective for me to get a point across. (Not even worrying about being politically incorrect.) From all the R-rated movies and who knows how many hours of MTV he's absorbed over the years, he's better at using combination varieties of the four-letter words. With my goodie-two-shoe background, I wouldn't attempt entering the ring by slinging curses with him. "Fudge" and "darn it" seem pretty pitiful if you're hoping to win a heated shouting match with a Boomerang.

What do you do when they've gone too far? And they will, they always do. Do you have the right to yell at adult children living at home? It's still your house and you're making the mortgage payments, you have the right to do most anything you want. Does it make you a bad post-parental unit yelling at them? (Bad is a very tenuous word in this concept.)

According to generic psychologists across the country, civilized adults must learn to "communicate" when there's a problem. Communicating is described as back and forth meaningful dialogue expressing your inner most feelings to one another; listening to the other and mirroring back what you heard. I don't think this works in a sterile textbook environment, let alone the real world.

Watch Dr. Phil on his talk show and you'll see what I mean. Dr. Phil's shows are about communicating issues and situations, and any adults having some relation to one another never seem to communicate well. Don't you love the man and his smooth way of putting out of control garbage into a nice neat little sack? It used to be you could check him out on *Tuesdays with Dr. Phil* on *Oprah*; it gave a whole new outlook to that day of the week for most women. Then some smart producer, probably Oprah herself, gave him his own show. He's becoming a whole feel-good and do-good industry. I'd like to bring him home to do an exorcism on my crowded, overstuffed house. Wrong, correct that, I'd rather be on his clean, quiet sound stage.

How many of you trump the Parent Card when you're trying to make a point? "I'm the parent. This is my house and my rules," sort of thing. Keep it in your wallet for emergencies only. That little piece of virtual plastic may come in handy some day. We don't know how many times you get to use the Parent Card with Boomerangs. There's fine print on the back stating "overuse of this card nullifies any power you may have accumulated in raising the little dickens." Over usage is not clearly defined, however.

You run into a variety of gray areas dealing with adult children at home. I'm not talking about ordinary gray blotches either. Try multi-car-pile-up gray or pea-soup-thick, San Francisco-fog-bank versions of grayness. Communication and power struggles are a classic can't-see-your-hand-in-front-of-your-face gray area. I'm talking the sound-a-foghorn kind.

Boomerangs learn, while out in the twenty-something reality world, from the Big Book of Dilbert-related communication tricks. Unless you've kept up with the comic strip of characters such as Dogbert and Wally, the non-descript chubby guy with glasses who lives in a cubicle, you've already lost ground trying to talk to your child. Our children's generation graduated cum laude of Partial Deafness Management Workshops and are fluently bilingual in double-speak answers. Corporate levels of brain washing attack our children the moment they sign the W-4 form towards independence, whether they work in retail, technical, or professional jobs.

Dealing with RAC's, who have been subjected to Catbert-twisted human resource concepts for any length of time, feels like trying to win an argument when your opponent's mouth is filled with mashed potatoes. You can't win if you can't understand a word they're saying. Fighting nonsense with logic creates major headaches and high blood pressure. They don't understand your exaggerated frustration since their response seems perfectly comprehensible to them. Sometimes you feel like lashing out "This is my house, damn it," and the only one who flinches at your tirade is the dog. What are the Boomerangs going to do, move out? I laugh.

We were young once. Doesn't always feel like it as we creak and groan rolling out of bed in the morning, but as youths of the Sixties, we were on a wild and sassy timeline. In long hair and mini-skirts we protested everything. Well, some of us did. I had a tough time giving up my bobby socks; I've always been comfort before fashion. Anti-establishment orientated, our generation battled against war and hate. And much of that was fought against our parents. We understand the need for being an individual.

We were the first generation to blast rock and roll by demand into the airwaves on both radio and television. Okay, they didn't have television before baby boomers, so we won that one by default. Our moms nearly fainted over Elvis and his hip gyrations; our fathers went purple with the first ear-splitting twangs of electric guitars. They bonded over the hair styles of the Beatles. We know about power struggles.

We smashed social conventions by living in communes or studio flats, with hordes of cockroaches for company—away from home. Let me repeat this most important phrase, we lived away from home. Oh, sure, we may have returned to lick our wounds once in a while from a nasty cutthroat divorce. But we made sure the transition was extremely temporary.

Moving home meant going back to the same old rules you ran away from as soon as you could. If you walked through your parents' screen door with a suitcase in your hand, it was back to keeping a curfew and no shoes on the furniture. Like stepping out of the colored visions of Oz and back into the black and white world of Kansas.

Our adult children, without a doubt, reap freedoms we fought hard for—they don't know it and they don't care. You want to talk about power struggles, try to start this conversation to get your point across. They don't have to wear horrible scratchy petticoats under god-awful dresses to school, or sit zombie like through church in a brother's hand-me-down suit jacket and tie every Sunday.

These new generations of adult children come back home whining and wounded because life didn't treat them fair. They have the nerve to cry about feeling disorientated, perpetually dissatisfied with everything in general and nothing in particular. Excuse me? Life isn't fair; no rose gardens or pot of gold at the end of the rainbow. I should know. Instead of living peacefully and enjoying my golden years, I'm back to Cub Scout meetings and Little League games every weekend with my grandsons. Don't even try to tell me life is fair.

The social culture wars of the Sixties, Haight Ashbury and Woodstock, or those of us who were ten miles behind the times with our noses in a book, triumphed over the preceding generation on the issue of whether we could sleep around or dress in any manner we felt comfortable. We created massive power struggles to break down barriers of hatred and racial prejudices.

Our generation made a lot of noise in the world, some about peace, and some about anger. When we left our childhood homes for college and careers, we took so much energy with us that thousands of books were written about the Empty Nest Syndrome.

Do our kids resent the notoriety of our youth? Is that what has driven them to create a syndrome of their own—the Crowded Nest Syndrome? Life is never good enough; they want everything that's ours.

The Gen X adults are adrift on an ocean of convenience, not as many parents demanding "shotgun" weddings telling them they have to settle down, or stick to a blue collar job they hate until retirement because it's what you're "supposed" to do. Of course, with all the disastrous hoopla of Enron and other Fortune-greedy corporations milking the workers dry of pensions or security, it's hard for anyone, even in our generation, to stay with a company more than ten years without facing layoffs or cutbacks.

By not forcing our genetic branches into the stereotypical restrictions we fought hard to break, these kids float along, indecisive, until stuck in a lethargic mode like gum on the bottom of their shoe, a twenty-foot wad of gum that paralyzes their whole forward movement. Procrastination becomes their coping strategy as they put off any thought of marriage or careers lasting longer than six months, and hang onto the creature comforts of their childhood home. Our creature comforts in our home we worked our butts off to obtain.

Kids today want to have their adult cake and eat it, too. Just because they've come home again, in their minds it doesn't mean we can treat them like children. Surprise! They will always be our children.

You wanted warm and fuzzy in the second half of your life. Every day you tried to face the world composed and with a smile, I'm sure. You organized your house in Feng Shui once the kids were gone, took classes in meditation to relieve all the adolescent angst they left behind, maybe exorcised the house with crystals and potions, like New Age Clorox and

Pine Sol. The results? A new and improved you.

Then one day after the adult children returned home you walk in your Feng Shui red door and before your foot is over the threshold, you're ready to punch their lights out for impromptu happy-hour parties, marathon telephone calls to the latest expensive Miss Telephone Psychic to find out their future, or (gasp) using up the last of the toilet paper without replacing the roll. Heaven forbid, they should actually step foot in a store and buy a replacement roll.

Feng shui does nothing to protect you from your own gene pool. Estrogen, highly needed, might have to be increased while they're around, but isn't strong magic. Take the little pills to minimize the night sweats and hot flashes. The kids are going to keep your cheeks flushed enough as it is.

Take control without taking up a baseball bat. I know you can do it. Remember, empower the parent without blowing a fuse. Needlepoint the saying on a good-sized pillow in soothing colors. Maybe in peacock shades of gem tones. Then beat the crap out of the pillow against the arm of your couch three hundred times, and you'll feel wonderful.

What are you going to get angry about when Boomerangs return? Aren't they perfect? They're your children; you raised them, and gave them life. Aren't they going to bow to your wisdom and experience?

Yeah, right, and you could be the next lottery winner. They are walking, breathing adults, or so their driver's licenses say—they want to be who they are and do what they want just as if they lived in their own apartment. Don't you wish they lived in their own apartment?

Irritating examples of too many people in one house may take place during the dinner hour when more than one person wants to use the kitchen or too many are trying to take a hot shower at the same time when the hot water tank will only handle one at a time.

When husband tries to steal all the hot water from you, you have repercussions, you cut him off in the bedroom, you burn his toast, oh that's right he likes carbonized food; okay, serve him white bread. But what if it's your RAC hogging the shower—you go to complain and you sound like a mom again, nagging, whining.

They act like their life is more important than yours, they'll use the excuse they have a job interview to go to—even though it's Saturday and everybody knows Human Resources never works on Saturdays. Give me a break.

Why would there be power struggles?

"I'm the mommy, that's why" won't work any more. They are taller; they've lived on their own for some time. You can't just send them to their room, but you don't want to be a prisoner in your room either.

You need to alleviate potential hazards as best you can. Take away any toys or edibles that will cause a tug of war between you. Don't buy just one dozen donuts if you know you won't get any by the next morning. Buy a dozen and a half and hide your share.

Don't plan on having a quiet evening at home if you know it's Tuesday and everyone wants to watch a monster truck special but you. Pick your strategies, pick your schedules, and you won't find as many pile ups during this rush hour on the freeway of life. It's an obstacle course you can beat if you keep an eye on the calendar, an ear to the ground, and a Hershey bar in your hand.

Don't let the frustrations get to you. Take a deep breath and exhale slowly; no, too fast and you're hyperventilating. Just inhale through your nose for three to four seconds, and then blow out gently through your mouth. No, not the whole thing in one rush, sounds too much like a sigh. Softly, gently.

Terrible two's—there's a phrase that brought fear to many a mother's heart when our kids were growing up. I'd up the stress ante by saying terrifying three's are worse. They're smarter, more opinionated and louder, having had a year's experience in temper tantrums. This critical stage of a youngster's life separates the women from the wimps. Crisis lines are set up for moms to call when raising these miniature volcanoes. 1-800-they-will-outgrow-it-if-you-live-through-it. Haagan Daas needs to come out with a special flavor just for moms of two and three-year-olds. Start with a vanilla or cream cheese base for something soothing, with bits of milk chocolate, maybe a few handfuls of cashews and almonds thrown in for protein, and finish with a swirl of caramel for a mentally nourishing treat.

Dealing with returning adult children is similar in frustration levels. Watch their thought processes. They want what they want, and they want it right now. They live here; they must own it. The brain of a RAC seems to send signals only part way through the gray matter process.

Don't try to argue with a three-year-old. It's tempting, but don't. Short people have not developed the crevices in the brain that say "oh, you're right, standing up in a shopping cart could lead to a nasty fall and brain damage." You expect your adult children, by their early twenties, to employ all the cul de sacs of their brain in daily life making decisions. Moving back home seems to revert their gray matter back to a three-year-old model.

"Didn't your father tell you to cut the grass before you went out?"

"But I just took a shower."

"And that happened before or after he told you to mow the lawn?"

"I needed a shower."

Stop yourself from opening your mouth, even if you have to bite the inside of your cheek and draw blood. It's a nasty cycle going nowhere. Like arguing with a three-year-old, arguing with an RAC is an exercise of futility and madness. Don't go there.

Another major reason to avoid power struggles is they lead to wrinkles. Like age and gravity aren't already against us in producing lines on our faces, engaging in battles with Boomerangs entrenches the worry lines in your forehead and deepens those between your eyebrows. Is winning a battle or two worth making those infuriating lines more pronounced?

My budget already holds twenty-to-fifty-dollars a month in beauty cosmetics and facials. Why don't they just give us a trowel and a jar of putty to fill in the cracks each morning? Something you might wash off at night, and re-apply every morning. Come on, if Hollywood can make AARP qualified movie stars look thirty again after sitting in a make over chair, why can't they share the process?

Wouldn't it be great if you could go into a Beautiful Faces, Inc. shop and have a new you created? Later you walk out with a shopping bag filled with thin pieces of rubber masking designed just for you to glue in place every morning.

You wouldn't mind going head to head with the Boomerang over issues once in a while when you looked like their younger sister. Just the shock factor when they first see you will gain you untold advantage in getting your points across. Revlon, are you listening?

When an RAC comes home with short people in tow, and one is three years old, you have a human nuclear melt down on your hands. Run away, hide while there's still time.

In our house we inherited a three-year-old with an adult child. Not just any thirty-pound three-year-old, one with a temper just short of Mt. St. Helen's and a vocabulary worthy of a politician. This multi personality being is radioactive material in a pint-sized canister. You never know when it's going to explode or how often. How can something look so sweet and innocent one moment and the next his head is spinning around? Faster than flipping a switch, he goes from I love you to I want to be adopted by real people who'll do as I say right now.

You think being older and taller than he is means something, but his lung capacity is twice the maximum strength of an opera singer. You haven't experienced the ultimate power struggle until you've lived with a three-year-old grandson. It's tug of war against a speeding locomotive, no, that's too tame. The rope is tied to a raging bull, and you're bare foot on broken glass. Cute as a button, but still a nasty, pissed off bull, and you're wearing nothing but red.

How did nature get that much power and fury in a package under three feet tall? He's got a switch somewhere you can trip without knowing it, like watching a space shuttle take off and you didn't hear the countdown.

Couldn't someone invent a warning sensory I can tape to his forehead to give me a five second head start before the explosion? I guess it's easier to make a device for predicting earthquakes than three-year-olds when they change gears.

We thought we had our hands full with his older brother during his terrible three's. Mere practices for us on a cheap merry go round. Dealing with the second one is an all out extreme roller coaster adventure with G force pain. Is it because we're older ourselves that makes it more exhausting dealing with antagonistic grandchildren or are these newer generations just coming out more complicated?

Scientists would be interested in the lung capacity of this guy. His vocal chords are flexible strands that reach frightening decibel levels. The Discovery Channel could do whole documentaries on him.

And because he's the little brother, he constantly chooses to mimic the older one in feats of daring and mayhem. I can't tell you how many conversations have started out:

"You can't play Little League baseball. You're only three years old."

"I can, too, I'm almost eight."

"You're almost four, and four-year-olds cannot play Little League."

"I don't want to be four, I want to be eight!"

The last line comes with emphatic foot stomping and intense glaring meant to turn you into stone. How quickly you go from beloved grandmother to the Wicked Witch of the West.

Miniature people come with their own built in power struggles. They fight the universe inside their souls throughout the day, every day. Your job is to stand by and help them not implode from the frustration. If big brother can ride a two-wheeler over a twenty-inch ramp, why can't he? No matter that you said no, he takes his training-wheel equipped bike over the edge of the jump and falls flat on his face in the driveway. Heart pounding screams can be heard in the next county, however not from blood shed or broken bones, but the pure preschool anger of not being able to fly through the air like his brother. How dare the universe stop him from succeeding? What evil gods thwart the mighty child from doing everything his big brother does? And god help you when you try to explain the difference between being eight and three to him for the four millionth time.

How about a Prozac laced Haagen Daas flavor of ice cream for three-year-olds? St. John's Wort laced chocolate chip cookies? Please. I need a truck full delivered tomorrow, express priority shipment. Come on, you guys could make a fortune here.

If I thought I was the grownup and should be able to call the shots in my own house, what a surprise lay ahead. Crowded nests call for a community attitude. You might win the decision of what's for dinner, and then lose the next three battles. Do you want to risk it?

Communal living aptly describes a household crowded with adult children. Not the peaceful communes of the Sixties with everyone pulling their share towards the common good. This is more like reality television. Think *Survivor* episodes, any of them, when you describe to your empty nester friends life at your house. Only no matter how many times you vote the adult child off your island, they're still there. Teams are drawn once they move in, the Generation X, Y and Zs against the Baby Boomers. Let the show begin.

Obstacle courses appear before you without warning. One morning you're climbing over mountains of dropped baggage and dirty clothes to reach the coffee pot, or you're crawling under the coffee table to reach sanctuary in the kitchen. Think of power struggles as treacherous quick sand, the more you flail about arguing, the faster you'll sink. Survival depends on staying calm and outsmarting the other side.

Each passing week makes the trials and exercises more trivial but complicated and demanding. Don't waste precious resources of energy in mud slinging and name-calling. Just mark your palm frond ballots with ash from the fire in your heart. Okay, there's no million-dollar prize for surviving life with adult children, but you can pretend. Any incentive to get up out of bed each morning works.

If you've never watched reality TV, think *Multiple Choices,* the new board game by Uncle Milton Fishing Price. You're living inside a dreaded driver's license quiz game with four different possibilities for every question, where every answer could be right, some more right than others, but only one is really right. If A sounds too strict and C sounds too lenient, B and D will be middle of the road. All of them could work, but only one wins the game. Easy if you've memorized the entire encyclopedia of US Highway Codes and Regulations. Sigh. It's never easy in a crowded nest—you never win or get all the answers right.

Take a concept, any concept, in physics or statistics, and you'll come up with a variety of possibilities sure to strain the strongest family ties. Here's an example. There are three cars in the driveway and three adults in the house. The Boomerang son's car breaks down because it's an ancient classic treated like a pinewood derby jalopy. Who ends up without a car for the next two days while it's being fixed? Who has to pay for the repairs? Isn't that amazing, the same person—me.

The universal explanation is he can't go out on a job interview if he doesn't have a car. Is there a job interview anywhere on the horizon? Probably not, but who wants to take the chance of leaving him stranded at home all day and listening to the broken recording "I would have had a job by now if I had used your car." Pretty much a no win situation.

Nothing like getting up an extra half hour to an hour early, usually in the dark of winter, scraping ice from a windshield, muttering oaths under my breath in puffs of steam to drive my husband to work so I'll have a car to get me to work. Gee, both of us are working, but we both can't have a car because the one who's not working might need one.

****

Pine Valley Library
09/12/2022 11:13:45   910-798-6392
AM
****

Automated Telephone Renewals
910-798-6320
Renew Online at
http://www.nhclibrary.org
****

Title
How to raise your adult children :
Author:
Parent, Gail, author. (DLC)n
80044597
Item ID: 34200010907356
Due: 10/03/2022

Title
The crowded nest syndrome :
Author:
Shaputis, Kathleen, author. (DLC)n
2001001242
Item ID: 34200007498187
Due: 10/03/2022

Fine Balance for $0.00
This Account

****

Pick your battles, people. A concept you learned back when the kids were pint sized and you knew trying to enforce certain ideals was a lot of hot air going nowhere. Do you want a clean room or a well-dressed child? Most days you couldn't have both and still have an ounce of strength left over for yourself. Pick your concerns, notions or contentions with stress levels in mind.

You can't make them get a job. I've seriously thought about copying down their social security number, practicing their signature, and filling out job applications for them. Pay back plot #325. After their high school pranks of signing your name to absence excuses or notes to get out of physical education classes, turn about is fair play.

I've tried circling possible job opportunities in the classified section of Sunday's newspaper with a big marking pen. Rarely works, they have an excuse for every situation. Why not take it a step further and do the paperwork for them? Wouldn't it be great to wake them up on a Monday morning and say, "Oh, by the way, you're expected at the foreman's office at Acme Hardware Warehouse and Slave Labor before 8 a.m." Lately, they have been guarding their wallets from me. I think they suspect I'm on to something.

What happened to the kids who would set up a lemonade stand at the drop of a hat to earn some money? Baby sit the neighborhood brats for hours on end enduring chewing gum in the hair and bruises on the shins before an evening was through? Oh yeah, that was me. Our generation wanted independence; we experimented with gainful employment in any way our age allowed. Newspaper routes, dog walking, baby sitting, we were creative in ways to earn money. In December did you ever sell mistletoe tied with red ribbon for ten cents a bunch door to door in your neighborhood? One summer I had a wagon full of avocados an uncle brought to our house from a tree in his yard, and I peddled them to the surrounding moms for a dime a piece or three for a quarter.

Who delivers your paper every morning? Some baby boomer that needs a second income to pay for the all people living in his house, right? I don't have an ambitious 13-year-old riding his bike and throwing the paper smartly to the porch. Mine is a scraggly faced, pitiful guy trying to stay one step ahead of the interest rates on his second mortgage. I feel his pain, but I envy his solitude in the car every morning.

Usually it's a senior citizen who asks "Do you want fries with that?" at our local fast food counter. The Boomerangs refuse to stand on their feet all day for minimum wage. Quite a few of these returnees made and lost fortunes in the dot com industry. Ask them to flip burgers? Pull-eeze. The seniors in many communities can't afford to live on their pitiful retirement checks and have to work for extra income. What's wrong with this picture?

I love the embroidered pillow, "Those aren't hot flashes, they're power surges."

When women talk about menopause, or for that matter professionals like doctors and printed health-topic pamphlets, the usual side effects come up like hot flashes, night sweats, and mood swings. Rarely do they talk about memory loss, and this side effect is a doozy. Maybe they can't remember to talk about it. Peri-menopause should come with a warning label that we interrupt this lifestyle with a *Short Attention Span Theater* marathon. Half the time I can't remember why I walked into a room. What was I going to do? I lose my train of thought from the time I get out of my chair and take the first three or four steps. Gone, all gone. I used to be able to back track what I had done during the day in locating my car keys or a book I layed down. I depended on that talent. Gone, all gone. It's enough to send me into a blinding white rage. Robbed of something very valuable to me when I wasn't looking. No one warned me it was going to be like this. And that's just wrong. With all the talk today of research towards Alzheimers Disease, you'd think just a little consciousness would be given to the fact that women get a taste of the problem right around this time in their lives. Be up front about it, forewarned is forearmed. Or something like that.

If you don't know it's happening, it can be a little scary, a touch of the dark side of life. Like your mind is going along and then someone hits the erase button and wipes out eighteen minutes of your memory. *Twilight Zone* music starts playing in the background and the little hairs on the back of your neck rise. Are there poltergeists following you around, moving your car keys and messing with your mind? It's a personal Watergate scandal and you're helpless to stop it.

Learn to carry a notepad with you everywhere, to make lists of what you want to do on any given day or reminders to yourselves. Some days it seems you need a post-it note to remind you to read your list. It's awful.

Add to this disappearing memory trick a houseful of people and you have the recipe for disaster. Not only can you not remember where you laid your car keys, but they've probably been moved a few times by borrowing Boomerangs. Looking for your black sweater you just washed? It could be in any number of locations after someone else uses it without your permission.

And that's just the older people. I have two grandsons who add their sticky fingerprints to most everything Gramma owns. Try to get a three-year-old to tell you where he left your camera, after climbing the bookshelf to get it and taking it heaven knows where to play. Or the disappearing cell phone, which you try to call, so the ringer can let you know where it is. But the child left it on and the batteries are dead, wherever it is.

Loss of memory during menopause is not lethal, it's the high blood pressure from frustration that'll get you. Combine this with returning adult children and you have to consciously take care of yourself or explode. Make an effort to put things (car keys, important papers) in the exact same spot every time. And woe to any human being that borrows the item and doesn't return it to the same place.

As for the physicians of the world, get the information on this side effect out there. Warn young women ahead of time while they still have the faculties to remember to do something about it.

At some point, the mixture of losing your short-term memory and enduring a crowded nest are going to clash into a quagmire. Late bill payments, losing your car keys. It happens. Too many people in too little space cluttering every flat surface in the house with stuff and papers is a recipe for chaos. Try to circumvent the frustration as much as you can and use chocolate as a bumper guard.

Remember, you have control over your emotions, thoughts, and reactions—probably nothing else in your life, just these. Take a deep breath, inhaling through the nose, one crowded nest, two crowded nests, three crowded nests. Now think soothing thoughts of shopping at the Mall of America all by yourself, with an unlimited gift card. That's it, now exhale through your mouth, slowly releasing the toxin of RAC's in the house. Two, three, four. Repeat the process, and with each breath think of the terrific bargains you find in each store. A perfect pair of shoes half off in one store, a great sweater that goes with everything you own in another, wtih an additional thirty percent off on the clearance rack in another store. Doesn't it feel wonderful?

Don't hyperventilate. Too much oxygen too fast just gives you a headache, and you don't always have the luxury of lying down with a cold, wet washcloth over your head.

Day jobs actually make a great hideout when you just don't have the energy to face the mass of humanity in your house. Jump in your car and commute to another world, a place where other adults show some respect for you. You get paid to make decisions. If the Boomerangs won't leave the house to get a job, you will. It's a matter of changing your attitude.

I've worked all my adult life. I started punching a time clock part time during the last years of high school and moved into full time the day after graduation. College wasn't discussed while I was growing up, you focused on working hard and making your way up the corporate ladder with dedication and busting your butt for your boss. This kind of concept is lost on many Boomerangs. Starting in the mailroom gets two thumbs down.

I bounced through a few jobs over the years, companies folded, departments were down sized—these are not just maladies of today—now they only make bigger headlines. The Seventies had their political and ecological scandals with big corporations that jeopardized whole communities while harboring no loyalty or respect for their employees. Pollution was a buzz word, smog was the daily weather forecast. The culprit? Big business.

After almost thirty years of pulling in a paycheck, I had the opportunity to stay home and be a full time writer for about thirty seconds. Before I could settle into my flannel jammies and fuzzy slippers at the computer, people began moving back into the house. Did the universe take out a full page ad declaring I was this close to fulfilling a dream? Were billboards posted along the freeway announcing to my kids that Mom was home alone? Probably a computer virus took one of my personal emails stating how excited I was to be able to stay home and write for once in my adult life and posted it on every chat room until my kids found out about it and ran home.

My boss doesn't believe I volunteer for overtime with the bald fact I'd rather stay late at the office than tangle with the bedlam at home. The company is located out in a forest, tranquil and serene. Commuting forty-five minutes each way is time to catch up on world news, find out the latest gossip, or listen to the Oldies station where the songs reflect a simpler time. Project problems on the job and irate customers are nothing compared to the free for all I can walk into after work.

I'm trying to wrangle a cot under my desk in negotiations with my next job review. I can wash up in the office bathroom and stay round the clock during the week. Maybe the family would appreciate me more if I show up only on weekends. One less body in the congestion of the hallway, but I don't want them thinking the house belongs to them either.

True, poverty forced me to get a day job once our humble abode became the main residence for most of our adult children. My first pathetic attempts at reading the employment classifieds again after my blink of freedom led to fits of raging temper tantrums. Why was I going back to work, when able-bodied twenty-something's were draining our provisions dry? I fought the irrational or rational concept for quite a while. Then I realized how quiet and soothing an office could be. People smile when I come in, they say please and thank you. I changed my attitude.

Power struggles come in various sizes and strengths. When you struggled as a young couple with bills, careers, and short kiddles running around the house, you dealt with continuing issues such as not enough hot water in the house. You staggered schedules of washing clothes or washing elementary aged beings that brought in a half pound of dirt and grass stains with them every night. The hot water tank never held enough to do everything for everybody every day. You were young and flexible. Sacrificing is one of the top ten parenting commandments. (Hmm, remind me I need to make up the ten commandments of post-parenting.)

You drew straws or played rock, paper, scissors over who showered at night and who got the morning. You turned the dishwasher on as you ran out the door with briefcase in one hand and kids with homework in the other. Some day you would have the house to yourselves and enjoy the luxury of hot water any time, any day without taxing your brain cells doing math calculations of how much the appliances had done and how many kids were left to send through the rinse cycle. We'd be older, wiser and earned the hot water tank all to ourselves.

Wrong, the RAC's come home and you find yourself fuming because for the second time this week, you were in the middle of rinsing shampoo from your hair when the water went frigid. Adding another adult body or two back into the schedule is enough to cause a massive power struggle over hot water, an incredibly precious commodity. Extra laundry, extra dishes, and more showers put a tax on your sanity when all you want is a nice hot shower after a long grueling day at work. (This is a moot point if you're still in the early stages of peri-menopause. Hot flashes like a cooler shower that is always ready, no waiting.) Hiding out in a hot shower is more likely to keep you from exploding on the adult child when your toast is burnt to a crisp because they've cranked the toaster to black and you like yours caramel brown. But they don't get it—they've used up all the hot water and killed your toast. And your point is? Power struggles.

Remember the exercises in the first chapter to detach yourself from a situation? When all else fails to avoid power struggles, reach into the refrigerator for a cold Skyy Blue and down two aspirins with it. Sort of a refreshing adult version of counting to ten. Use this plan sparingly, though, you want to watch the number of calories consumed. Don't gain weight just to avoid an argument with the tall ones. That's adding another problem to the mix instead of lightening the load or stress.

You don't want to sound like a nagging mother all the time. It strains the vocal cords and enhances those wrinkles in the forehead. Post-parenting is about relaxing the strangle hold of having to critique, check up on, and oversee the various lives and issues in the home. Yet, try to get across the idea that this is your home and they need to plan on leaving soon, and you start repeating certain phrases, parroting many of the same noises you made when they were smaller. It's an easy trap to fall into, as they tend to act like children instead of adults while in the house. If they can't act like adults, you tend to step back into the parent role to get anything accomplished.

Pick your battles—stay one step ahead of the RAC's. If you know it's Thursday and you have your Must See TV shows coming up, remind the other people in the house. Two or three times if you have to. Don't expect them to remember squat. It won't happen. Post flyers around the house, "Mom out of order—8 p.m. to 11 p.m." Order a pizza in for yourself and bar the bedroom door while you settle in for a few hours of escapism.

The more you scheme and dream ahead, the fewer power struggles you'll run into with Boomerangs. You can do this. A little more effort now will save a lot of blood pressure medication in the future.

Bottom line, my all time favorite way to avoid the migraines of power struggles with the RAC's—doubling my prescription of Prozac. If you don't have one, get one. How you made it this long without one is beyond me, but why suffer any longer? Returning adult children aren't worth more gray hairs and deeper stress lines.

4

His, Yours, and Migraines

Whether it's one of his fair-haired children who comes home, or my genetic bi-product from a previous marriage, does it make any difference whose overgrown kid it is? They're a pain in the butt no matter what side of the gene pool they descended from.

Half of the post-parenting situations in the country exist with the returning adult child belonging to both parents. You got married out of college or high school, had children and for good or bad, they returned home to the nest. You each have equal parts of genetic make up invested in the kid and can soothe your frazzled soul with the support of each other during this difficult situation. You both remember what a fussy child he was, or what hot buttons not to push. You share the past twenty-some years together and know the best and worst of your child.

The other half of us are dealing with additional layers of emotional issues and past baggage being a blended family. Course we could use it as a whining excuse, too.

Not everyone in the Sixties and early Seventies took their marriage vows the distance. Some ran into political differences like women's lib forcing a break up. Or you ended up blowing your nose on the poetic vows you wrote on pink tissue paper. How could you have known when you married your soul mate in the middle of a field of daisies, you'd be allergic to daisies?

With current divorce rates claiming half the marriages there stands a good chance you will be dealing with an additional his or yours concept to your crowded nest. Dealing with the explosive and paralyzing yours, mine, and ours syndrome in addition to that of Boomerang children encourages you to create a few extra rules. Don't let guilt gild the situation, you're done paying for braces and piano lessons or court mandated child support payments.

When both his and yours come back to the nest in crisis at the same time run, do not walk, to the nearest warehouse store for the large economy size jar of Tylenol PM and just put yourself in a coma. More than one adult child at home is a 24/7 headache you don't want to experience.

I can take that nightmare one step further having two RAC's living under my roof, with one of them bringing grandchildren back with her.

Do I know more about Power Rangers and *Blue's Clues* than anyone else my age? You betcha, except those women who delayed maternal gratification and traveled all over the world first, owned mega companies and conglomerates, and had their first child at 45. I'm mistaken for one of them all the time.

What do I get for knowing all this trivia? Nothing. I come home after a long, tiresome day at work and find two young grandsons with their arms crossed over their chests and two oversized dogs waiting for me in the driveway. What a welcoming committee. Both pint-sized darlings won't shut up, as they scream over the voice of the other telling you about their day's activities, not to mention two slobbering masses of fur who won't leave you alone period. One chocolate colored tail is beating my thighs black and blue or body slamming into me as the boys try to get their fair share of attention. Think any other adult in our house would play ball or catch with them? Dream on. Can't I just come home sometime to an empty house where I can relax with an ice cold Diet Coke and not share half the can with a bunch of runny nosed little people?

Gramma's the hip one, watching animated marathon television with a boy on either side of me and dogs at my feet every evening.

What has happened to all our American cartoonists? Did we leave the import doors open too long letting in hours and hours of *Pokemon, Digimon,* and more? Hubby is caught up in the Asian cartoon soap opera *Dragonball Z.* The man had the nerve to harass me about my few years of enjoyment watching NBC's *Days of Our Lives* when he is glued to the television set every evening with the rest of the household, watching colored silicon slides of bad acting and worse dialog from action characters with names like Goku. Hubby claims his addiction is 'bonding time' sitting in the living room with two grandsons on his lap all eyes glued to the television. They argue over what will happen next. White sticky rice version of television, if you ask me.

At least I've an excuse for my affection towards John Black and the citizens of Salem. From late 1993 to early 1995, my mother lived with us bed-bound in our living room until she passed away. Her favorite daytime soap was *Days*; she loved the more police-related storylines and plot twists. The woman would have made a great crime detective. When I was growing up she could spot details out of place and unknown fingerprints a mile away.

My work schedule back in 1994 included ten-hour days Monday through Thursday, so every Friday found me home and watching the hour-long daytime drama with her. I got hooked. It happens. I watched it for a few years after, keeping her memory close to me, knowing she'd probably be thinking of the characters and actions, what with Brady and Belle grown up and Craig and Nancy joining the cast. I love Nancy's feistiness. 'Course, Mom knows what's going to happen already.

As my mother and grandmother before me, I worked fulltime for a living straight out of school and missed any daytime television soap opera interest. I had a brief interlude from employment right after my daughter was born and watched hours of the Mike Douglas variety show during the week (not the actor married to Catherine Zeta-Jones), the entertainment predecessor to Oprah and Rosie. Still I never got involved in any kind of loyalty to soap operas.

After sitting with Mom and watching the antics and dramas of the citizens of Salem, I do understand the drawing power. No matter how crazy and chaotic your life gets, the characters in a soap opera make yours seem like easy street. For a brief hour you worry about someone else's problems and crises. *Days* isn't so much bed hopping as it is cat-fighting among the fashionable women, Salem police dealing with kidnappings, crimes of the heart and of the street, and a few bizarre twists in the story lines due to Stephano's or the latest villain's shenanigans.

Daytime Prozac. You don't think about your family's warts and moles when you're concentrating on *Days*. And their story lines take forever. Granted, this drives a best friend of mine absolutely nuts, an empty nester who wants things to happen one, two, three. She only endured it for my sake when I came over during my lunch hours for a visit in 1995. A pregnancy on *Days* can take up to two years. I have enough trauma in my life going snap, snap, snap. I like easing along someone else's problems.

So when flipping through the channels one day (and the fact that I had the remote in my hand alone was a miracle), champagne bubbles and polka music came on, and it felt like mental pabulum washing over me, warm, creamy oatmeal on a snowy day. The well-known cast of people singing and dancing looked young and vibrant in color-coordinated outfits of chiffon and satin. I felt like a child again, stretched out on the rug with my homework scattered around me. A time of less stress and less ugliness in the world. Just ABC, Lawrence Welk's syrupy music, and myself. Can you remember the innocence of the Lennon Sisters quartet, and former Mouseketeer Bobby and his partner waltzing their hearts out with graceful choreography week after week?

Okay, it's televised saccharin. I'll do it again if I have the chance. I know myself. The grandkids will pull down the blinds and lock the doors making sure the rest of the world doesn't find out their gramma has gone off the deep end. Sssh, don't tell them.

Long ago and far away when I first met him, husband was a weekend dad, picking up two boys every other weekend and plying them with adventures and carnivals, hot dogs and videos for two full days.

The round trip back on Sundays started out filled with the Dr. Dimento radio show on full blast, and everyone singing off key to the crazy lyrics. The last half of the drive was more solemn as hubby licked his wounds caused by saying good-bye for another two weeks.

Spoiling wasn't the nature of the game back then for hubby and sons. More like the Hardy Boys at a forty-eight hour workshop for male bonding, but without a lot of rules. Cold leftover pizza for breakfast, after falling asleep past midnight watching a stack of rented videos. That was the usual fare. The living room turned into a campground with sleeping bags and dirty clothes mapped across the floor. Bags of Cheetos and various half-filled soda cans dotted the far corners. A manly feast.

During the summer, long weekends driving to the Colorado River visiting grandma and grandpa added to their list of things to do. Over the years photos and slides of bronzed boys attest to fun memories.

By the time I entered the picture, the three of them were very comfortable in this schedule. Certain rites of passage occur between a man and his sons whether they live together full time or not, the latter taking longer. But love holds them fast no matter how many days they physically live apart due to marital circumstances. The three Caballeros.

Fitting into the triangle as a stepmother, I tried not to stomp too heavily on their fragile male bonds. Two weekends a month were okay but not enough for any of them—and adding another person to the mix helped in some ways, hindered in others. You try not to be so much a wet blanket, as an anchor to their all-male family.

My contributions to this clan were encouragement, planning, and scheduling events on the calendar. Make sure food was prepared or picked up along the way, cutting a few corners giving the threesome more time together. It couldn't be easy for the boys to know I got the lion's share of their father's attention while they were gone.

And it's not something I've discussed with them now that they are grown men. I look back at our wedding video with two shining faces acting as our ushers, the oldest walking my mother down the aisle and the youngest walking my mother-in-law to her seat. Both smiling anyway. Was it for the camera's sake or did they truly okay the union? Hmm, remind me to check one of these days when the house is empty. It's been fifteen years, and we're all still around together—must have done a few things right in helping to cement the future.

Fast-forward and here we are in a new house, new state, and new neighborhood and hubby's invited the oldest son to move in with us before I've unpacked a third of the moving boxes.

"You did what?"

"Asked him to live with us. I'll get him a part-time job. He'll love it here."

"Here. As in our house?"

"Of course, he doesn't have any savings since his mom kicked him out of the house."

"And you don't see the reason behind this? She may have had just cause to shove him out of his too-comfortable mode?"

"It's a fresh start for the kid. It'll be fine. Look, here he comes." A yellow rented moving van pulled up to the curb.

Funny, the van is yellow but brilliant red flashing lights are going off in my head.

Small gratitude lives in the back of my throat that the youngest son hitched himself to the Army and a new wife. The service has kept him off our doorstep for a few years. Hubby is pleading for the second son to get the Army to transfer the whole family to Fort Lewis, just a few miles up the freeway. The hamster wheels are turning in that brain of his, how to get all his chicks back to the roost.

Father and oldest son, my two overgrown Baby Hueys, tend to make up for lost time by spending hours in the garage chatting about transmissions and carburetors, car stereos and speakers. Long Saturday mornings find the daring duo at the local Pick-a-Part salvage yard looking for buried treasures. All well and good, right? Keeps both out of the house, I can turn off a few TV's, open a few windows.

Except, and it's a big exception, these two talk each other into major projects having to do with cars and boats costing hundreds and hundreds of dollars. Not a twenty-dollar bill here and there as it was when the boys were little and a few video games and an ice cream entertained them; we're talking mega-bucks. It's chrome this and rebuilt that, none of which seems to be needed as much as "wouldn't it be cool if" between the two of them, and the checkbook deflates like a balloon with a fast leak.

I don't have a husband and a twenty-something stepson at this point, I have two teenagers sneaking off to buy heaven knows what with checkbook and credit cards in tow. I end up being a nagging crabby mother to both of them. That's not right. Where's the other post-parenting partner? He's melted into a bowl of guilty post-weekend father mush.

"What do you think you're doing?" I hiss at hubby through clenched teeth.

"What? Making up for lost time," he says. The magic words to make me back off with visions of warm fuzzies dancing through my head.

"Right. That's the third piece of greasy equipment you've dragged home this month. I think the kid gets the message."

"What message? Oh, yeah, right—uh, honey, can I have the checkbook back? We need to go to the auto parts store."

Like if the two of them decided to tackle me for it I'd have a chance. We're talking six hundred pounds of testosterone.

Male menopausal pleasure is gleaming all over his face. The oldest son is in the roost.

My computer becomes a gang-related weapon as both of them sit there side by side looking up accessories, serial numbers, and anything else they can get in trouble over. I call it the sucking-up-to-the-adult-child gang. Admission expensive. No women allowed.

While hubby is getting all the glory for being the best dad in the world, providing room and board, great weekend adventures in Pick-a-Part land, oozing in Tom Sawyer and Huckleberry Finn rites, I become every clichéd wicked stepmother (WSM) story you can imagine. I worked hard in the beginning years of our marriage never to fall into the negative trap. I supported those years of weekend visits. I compromised my plans to make sure the WSM image didn't come across in the boys short term visits with dad. I was a mom; I knew the ins and outs of what constituted a nasty WSM persona.

Today welcome to WSM Central, every day in every way I'm on a wicked rampage. I find twice the number of wet towels on the floor in two different bathrooms. Like father, like son is not my favorite saying. How did the theme song from Patty Duke go? "They walk alike, they talk alike." Well, if not, that's how mine goes. Two bookends of over-sized male species from the same tree, sharing double and triple x clothes, and killing me financially in dollar and cents.

No more Ms. Nice Guy. I get zero support from the weekend dad\now fulltime father. The kid is old enough to be a father now and doesn't need to have his meat cut up for him. Meow.

And remember the job hubby promised him if he moved up here? Well, it lasted a whopping few months. Granted, the company changed the rules about having family members working anywhere in the organization. But months of minimum unemployment ran out and nothing happened. A part-time job here, another one there for a while was all the kid undertook, giving him some extra pocket money. Our budget with the additional strain stretched paper-thin over time, finally burst into shredded pieces trying to sustain all of us.

An ugly stiff mask took over my face. I shoved forty pounds of negative emotions down my throat instead of letting them erupt, and they went straight to my thighs.

The refrigerator in the garage holds a case of various Miller beer products on Thursday, but over the weekend it's gone between the two of them and the son's new friends and comrades.

Do I get any benefits like having yard work done? Does anyone check the oil in my car while they're out with heads together under a hood? Of course not. Too simple of an idea—make up for a little of the inconvenience and stress I'm being dealt. Yes, I ask for chores to get done, I state my wants bluntly, nothing. I've made the obvious known in capital letters more than a few times around here. Never worked, but I'm getting used to banging my head against the proverbial brick wall. A few more times and I will probably start to hear classical music from the ringing in my ears.

Notice the animated Disney classics all show the wicked stepmother dealing with a pale princess of some sort, Snow White and Cinderella come quickly to mind. Where's the story of the WSM of a male child? Zero, zilch, nada. Not having a fairy tale role model, I made up the spitting and cursing all by myself.

Ahh, isn't it cute, the real fairy tale of the 21ˢᵗ century—father and son living together making up for lost memories. I'm watching the animated sub-titled version where my savings account drops faster than the NASDAQ points with this reunion.

In talking about his, yours, and migraines, is there a difference when one or the other comes home to roost? Not in my house. Hubby invited, encouraged, summoned both of them to "come on up." I can be equally or doubly pissed at him as time wears on. We have one Boomerang each under our roof—both arrived on the front doorstep with hubby's personal invitation in hand. What am I to do with the spousal frustration over this paternal nesting monster?

People ask me why I didn't make this chapter his, mine, and ours—like the adorable movie with Lucille Ball and Henry Fonda. Both widowed, they married each other and united something like twelve kids between them, and she ends up pregnant. Rather a sick comedy, don't you think?

Due to physical restrictions officially named a hysterectomy back in my mid-twenties, all my baby plumbing is gone, thank goodness. If I get pregnant, my photo better be on the cover of the *National Enquirer* as "Miracle Conception Rocks the Pope." Hubby and I married knowing there would never be a child of our loins. We saved towards the day when the kids we had grew up and left us our paychecks to use as we wanted.

We didn't have high hopes of being mega rich in retirement, scaling Mt. Everest, or touring the world in our own motor yacht. Well, husband wants (past, present, and future tense) that last one really bad, not a sailboat a motor yacht. Nasty rumor during our first years of being married was we were retiring on a boat in our future.

"Honey, check out this thirty-six foot cabin cruiser," hubby's favorite line at the four hundredth boat show he's drug me to. "Wouldn't this be perfect for us?"

"Perfect for what?"

"Our golden years. We'll sell the house and live on the high seas. We putter from Mexico in the winter to Alaska in the summer. Maybe a side trip through the Panama Canal for Christmas." The man's eyes go glassy around this part. I've lost him to the sound of distant waves slapping against the side of an imaginary boat.

I hate water. I get claustrophobic getting my face wet in the shower. And the man, who claims to love and adore me, pledged his heart to me in front of a minister and our friends, plans to stick me on a floating piece of wood? I don't think so.

This chick will wave from shore if he wants to wander off like Christopher Columbus on the Sinking Leena. I'll keep a light on in the window like a personal Motel 6 for him to find his way back to dry land. My idea of living this dream is just to put on a CD of ocean sounds, breaking waves, and seagulls. Close enough for me. I've gotten better about my water phobia. But I'm staying on good ol' terra firma.

We were young, retirement was down the road, and we focused on saving towards some peace and quiet. Oh, the plans we made, visions of Cabo San Lucas—we were crazy enough in 1993 to buy a time share down there in sunny Baja, California, thinking we would spend a couple of weeks a year soaking up sun and surf. Ha, silly mortals, Fate laughed behind our backs.

My version of the "ours" in that Lucille Ball movie title turned out to be the first grandson. A little entity born into our house and took roots in our hearts. We changed diapers, watched USC football games on Saturday afternoons with this sleeping infant in between us and realized our lives were never going to be the same.

We didn't plan to raise another generation, but we're not doing too badly. Let me qualify that no one planned on him staying with us as long as he has. His mom is my daughter, and over the years financial black clouds followed her through one crisis or another. In the beginning the little guy stayed with us a few months at a time. Things happen. Then more happened, and he's still here.

The oldest grandson is a prime candidate for a politician. He's good looking, personable, and charms the money off most adults he meets. He can schmooze a quarter or dollar off someone with a few choice words and you don't realize it's happened. It'll be interesting to see which party he ends up representing. The adults in the house are equally divided between Democrat and Republican. Maybe he'll create his own party.

Hubby and I haven't been on a romantic vacation in years, since we've become grandparents actually. Our finances are in a sorry state, with ump-teen tall and short people living on our paychecks. It will be decades before we splurge on fanciful and romantic trysts in far away lands. At this point, overnight at a cheap motel is grounds for a Harlequin novel backdrop.

Makes for a bitter pill when the mail arrives one day and the oldest adult son received letters from his mom with foreign postmarks all over the envelope. She's enjoying her freedom and empty nest, must be nice. Okay, I didn't have plans of traipsing across Europe; it's not on my top ten list of things to do. But when the letters and postcards show up, along with other friends enjoying rested vacations on foreign soil, it smacks across the face that other post-parenting people are out there having a great time while I'm paying for room and board for these kids.

People my age, you know who you are—we don't have to give out numbers in this book—are well versed in the finer tastes in life. We are Baby Boomers, hear us roar. We share a subscription to *People* magazine and watch, read, listen to the news with CNN, The Times and NPR radio. We're in the know about the good and the bad, the evil and the blessed in the world. We know the difference between sushi and raw fish.

Then one day I'm not just a Baby Boomer but also a grandmother. Add hours of watching mind numbing Nickelodeon and Cartoon Network and you have my world. A few perks come with the job as Gramma if you keep your wits about you. I had to watch old videotapes of the *Mighty Morphin Power Rangers*, circa 1994, over and over and over, teenagers in primary colored spandex fighting cheap plastic-molded bad guys. One special hunk, Tommy, the original green ranger and then famous white Mighty Morphin Power Ranger, made the hours not nearly so painful a journey. (Hmm, then in later years he became a red ranger.) Have you seen this guy? He's gorgeous, polite, muscular, did I say gorgeous? He's a nice guy with long hair, in tight spandex, helping to rescue the world from phony Japanese villains.

My oldest grandson discovered this kung-fu teeny-bopper group years after the original Power Rangers moved on to bigger and better career choices. But by the magic of used videos we found at yard sales and antique stores, Tommy came to live in our television. Youngsters don't comprehend the fickle finger of popularity. If they see the show on television, again the difference between video and cable connection means nothing to short people, it must be real and it must be current.

Power Rangers are an ever-evolving species. How can a grandmother keep up with Zeo, Light Speed Rescue, and more, each with its own theme song and weaponry? Thank goodness for eBay.com, a lifesaver when trying to buy that special Ranger toy when it's been off the market for six years. I recently saw a special episode where they brought back the last ten Red Ranger characters to battle together against evil. Gramma had to watch Tommy help save the world one last time.

Another love in my life besides Tommy was Steve of *Blue's Clues*. Day after day, video after video, Steve came in and sang the rules to playing *Blues Clues* until everything I saw in real life could be described in three simple clues. Not surprisingly, Steve made *People's* top 50 bachelors one year. A joy to his own mom (I'll bet he didn't come home to roost—in fact he could buy her a whole new hen house), and thousands of grateful mothers of preschoolers everywhere, he should make a great husband and father some day.

A few years later I got another new grandson and the enchantment of Blue returns with a vengeance. Steve sang to us in the car from the cassette player with auto rewind or whatever the control is called to let the tape play continuously, non-stop, until you turned off the engine or drove off the edge the cliff. The plastic cover for the tape broke in the first couple months, but it didn't matter, the tape never left the machine if I wanted peace and harmony in the car.

I bought a new car (when the RAC's wore out my other one), and it came with a CD player—in the back of my mind I foolishly think I'm going to move on without Steve and Mailbox singing "oh so happy." Wrong. Interesting, you don't just listen to the entire montage when you use a CD for the three-year-old. The little guy knows you can repeat a single track on a CD, he has a player next to his bed where repeated chorus's of Backstreet Boys dance in his head. You get in the car, push the Repeat button on the first song, and your brain becomes curdled mush before you get to your destination.

Six years of *Blues Clues* have past. See why Steve is part of the family? I lived with him serenading me more than Michael Bolton and Barry Manilow put together. So I'm shocked to find out when flipping through a magazine at the doctor's office (to get a refill of my Prozac) a full-page ad about a new kid coming onto the show to take Steve's place. Joe. Who's Joe? The folks at Nick Jr. handled the passing of the blue baton with grace and gentleness. Joe is Steve's younger brother, and he comes to take care of Blue and friends while Steve goes off to college.

Not like what we endured as preteens back in the Sixties when they dumped Dick York from *Bewitched* and threw in a new Darrin. How traumatic was that? One week Samantha is married and kissing the adorably kooky Darrin with knobby knees, and the next week this stranger had his arms around her. Were we going to come home from school and find our dad replaced?

I haven't watched an entire evening news program for the last seven years. Everyone from adult kids to the grandkids and hubby are addicted to *Dragonball Z* during dinner. By the time we're through catching up on pre-school antics and third grade lessons in math and spelling, I'm ready for bed.

I'm eight or nine issues behind in reading my *People* magazines. There's zero reading time in a crowded nest. I can't sit in the bathroom for half an hour like hubby. A) My other cheeks get cold because hot flashes never seem to reach that far. B) As soon as the door closes, the phone and/or doorbell rings. C) The dogs and boys are banging against the door demanding attention. Who can concentrate reading the latest Hollywood gossip with all that racket? Where's the Tylenol?

5

R-E-S-P-E-C-T

Don't even think about getting any action in the boudoir during a crowded nest situation. If you were inhibited between the percale sheets when the kids were little, try getting hot when you know they know what goes on behind closed bedroom doors between consenting adults. And they know you know they know so they expect you to act like Mr. and Mrs. Cleaver with separate twin beds and buttoned-up pajamas. Respecting yourself and your spouse physically, sexually, romantically, perversely even more so when Boomerangs come home is darn right difficult.

Viagra, schmagra. Having adult children at home chills any middle-aged active hormones worse than a cold shower. You dreamt of a time when the two of you would be alone in the house. Sexual fantasies of reverting back to newlywed energy kept us alive. Fantasies of a time where comfort and fun meant wearing less clothing and getting a little at odd hours of the weekend, enjoying the vivid colors of our sensual sunset years.

When you're young and raising your family you plan sexual dates with your spouse. You check your calendars, make arrangements for the kids to sleep over at someone else's house, and keep your fingers crossed that none of the kids come down with the flu and neither of you throws his or her back out before the big night. It's part of being a parent, and you endure the hassle because you know one day they will grow up and leave home.

You look forward to spontaneous attacks of lust. Doesn't have to be often, no matter what your husband tries to tell you, but if you get in the mood to play sex goddess on a Saturday afternoon, there should be fewer obstacles to jump over.

The hard work of juggling hormones and schedules should be over once a family is raised; it's time to play again. Albeit, this is what got you into the mess of parenting in the first place; the good news is by this time there is less chance of a surprise visit from the stork. Enjoy lust for lust's sake.

While you're waiting for the chance to have sex again (it could be weeks or months in a crowded nest), do your keigle exercises. Who comes up with these names? Dr. Keigle's family voted to change their last name after serious articles were written about exercising your "happy place." You know what keigles are, don't you? The muscles between the legs that we can restrict and release to help with bladder control and vaginal enjoyment.

Might as well try to keep the area as tight as possible for our age, in case some day we are alone with hubby. Keigles can be done anywhere, in the car driving to the supermarket, laying in bed just before you go to sleep or wake up in the morning. Make signs for yourself that say DYK, "do your keigles," and leave them on the dashboard of the car or the bathroom mirror. The adult children will think you've gone around the bend and joined a middle-aged cult; that's okay.

Then right after doing those you might as well throw in a few isometric exercises and tighten the tummy muscles. Heck, we don't have a lot of better things to do with the adult children hanging around the house. Suck in your stomach muscles as much as you can and hold for ten seconds, counting Crowded-Nest-Syndrome-One, Crowded-Nest-Syndrome-Two and then release. These have the same benefits as sit-ups, sort of the portable version of exercise. Do these anywhere, anytime to flatten the maternal tummy—the flab we inherited from birthing the adult children. The gift that keeps on giving.

If you think coming out of the bedroom together is bad, adult children know what you've been doing if you both come out with wet hair. Taking a shower together is not something our generation invented, these kids have probably been there, done that themselves, and we just ruined their appetite. Okay, that would be a good thing, if we saved a couple of dollars in groceries. Enduring the wrinkled prune look on their face takes longer.

If I want sex, I have to pay for a hotel room to get any privacy from the family. It's worse than trying to hide sex from your parents. What is it with hotels lately? If you do spring for a night somewhere, you only get from 4 p.m. to 11 a.m. which amounts to something like $20 an hour for sex (one or both of you end up sleeping through most of the reserved room time.) This is highway robbery. 'Course, again, you take privacy where you can get it and Tom Bodett did say he'd leave the lights on for us if the call of the wild strikes. Hotels are expensive—use this sparingly. Do the hotel clerks look at you funny, when you ask for only one night? At our age? Nah.

Kissing your spouse can be a bone of contention to the younger grandkids. The three-year-old goes on and on about how his Papa kisses his Gramma and one night they went to a party and were dancing. The kid has a great memory, because it happened only one night at a Christmas party, and we've heard about it for six months.

If it's difficult trying to be amorous under the same roof with adult children, add grandchildren to the mix and the birds and the bees will die off for lack of privacy. You're back to square one with short people in the house having rabid curiosity and zero patience.

"Gramma, you're a girl?"

"Yes, I am."

"And Papa's a boy?"

"When a boy gets that tall, you call him a man."

"And you kiss Papa?"

"As often as I can."

"Why do you want to do that?"

Doesn't it seem like yesterday you were explaining the birds and the bees to your children? And now their children are living with you with the same nosey attitudes!

Oedipal complexes rear their ugly heads before you know it. An innocent kiss good-bye to your spouse before you go off to work can set a toddler into a tailspin. You find yourself looking over your shoulder to see if you're alone before you step into his arms for an embrace.

And when I say alone, I'm including the dog. With so many people in our house, even the dog gets jealous when I try to spend a moment hugging my own husband, whom I haven't seen close up in over ten days. We pass in the hallway once in a while or wave across the crowded living room during the weekends, but by nightfall I'm usually unconscious before he comes to bed. No use waiting up for him. If we're both inside the bedroom, the three-year-old sits just outside the door, and if he hears us, the bedroom door bursts open with him shouting, "What's going on without me?"

I'm dying from his adoration. A miniature guard dog, ready to bite any ankle, defending my honor against male intrusion. Should I feel flattered or petrified?

I think a romantic post-parenting rendezvous should start with a variety of candles burning in the bedroom. My body's not as tight as it once was, I don't want bright lights accentuating the additional love handles or inches accumulated over the years. Freckles and age spots dot the landscape of my bare skin that once sported tan lines and curves. I haven't looked in a mirror to see the backside of myself in fifteen years; I'm not about to spoil the record. Soft flickering candles are more than enough glow. Be romantic—maybe scatter rose petals on the bed and soft Kenny G music on the stereo. No rush, no tension. Foreplay can last longer than the Kentucky Derby when it's just the two of you.

Nice if you can manage it. With umpteen people at our house, I think we're scheduled for sex twice in the next five years.

I'm beginning to understand women who covet their romance novels. No CNS sufferers in those books. The heroine may have to endure torture and deception before the good guy finally kisses her, but she doesn't have to worry about her adult children hearing the bed squeak.

Day dreaming through romance novel concepts and coveting Chippendale posters are usual side effects of CNS. Young strapping box boys at the local grocery store begin to catch your eye. Magazine ads for men's cologne are enough to set the hormones discussing possibilities. Not that anything physical is going to happen. You're just thinking about it.

Your house is too crowded.

The car's too small.

You can't afford a hotel.

And your parents either live with you or in a retirement home, so you can't borrow their place.

I say friends should help friends. If you've got a spare guest room, offer it to the CNS sufferer. Take your spouse out of the house for a long Sunday brunch and leave fresh towels behind in the bathroom. Donating a couple of hours a month to a desperate couple is like releasing positive auras back into the world. The CNS sufferer will be truly grateful for the opportunity, and promises to change the sheets before they leave. You never know when you might be in the same overcrowded situation, and need the favor returned. Heaven knows, I would open a bed and breakfast for my fellow CNS sufferers if the situation were different.

My idea of romance any more is a king-sized bed with a mattress warmer and heavy dark curtains, keeping any sunlight out for about thirty-six hours, to let me sleep straight through. Touch me and die. Don't even think about encroaching on my side of the bed, either. I want my own space to stretch or curl into the fetus position if I want to without bumping into another body. Lust still flows in the rusty veins of my loins. (Do I have loins?) I'm not anti-sex. I'm just menopausal and don't see why I have to use up precious minutes of pure blissful sleep by getting poked and sweaty.

Is this Mother Nature's idea of a sick joke, having the guy pass out immediately after sex into a coma deep enough to render him useless for hours and women are wide awake. I thought she was on our side; she's a mother for goodness sake. After orgasm the guy falls asleep and the woman might as well clean the house, cook a seven course meal, or find the international cure for hiccups because her body and mind aren't going to let her sleep, no way, no how. It's inhumane. Give me afternoon delights or leave me alone. I'm not staying up all frigging night because of sex.

I have a gorgeous hunk of a guy; don't get me wrong. Hey, that's why he's still around after inviting all these people home. Didn't you know? He's the one who left the door unlocked. He picked up the phone and invited them, pleaded with them. The man called southern California two or three times a month, after successfully getting adult son up here, to convince adult daughter to move in with us. Oh, sure, he'll give you a convincing song and dance about how it took daughter being laid off from her travel-related job due to the horrors of 9/11 before she'd move. Something about 75% of her office being let go and a drastic drop in tourism—all I know is he happily rented a truck and brought back tons of furniture and every knick knack and souvenir shot glass she had on her walls.

At my age, I don't need a lot of time and atmosphere for gratification. Props and frivolity would be nice, but I'd take an hour of quiet solitude in being able to stretch out naked with hubby any day over restrictive lace, fuss, and fanfare. Back in the old days, somewhere between Adam and Eve and Tom Cruise, if you wanted sexy lingerie, you usually bought it from the Fredericks of Hollywood catalog. Insanely skimpy outfits in three hot colors (red, black or white) consisted of a yard of lace and a string or two, guaranteed to bring joy to your significant other's face. Thank goodness you only had to wear those scratchy, miserable things for about three seconds. You turned him on and they came off. Everything wearable was constructed in peek-a-boo designs, with nothing covered and nothing left to the imagination. You could order French maid or leopard skin designs for variety. After a night or two of horny passion they stayed waded up in an underwear drawer.

Kids came along. That nonsense ended.

Well, I did order a pair of white spandex jeans one year for Christmas. Those were the most comfortable pants, almost an iridescent white. They looked sprayed on, which meant they were not supposed to be worn during daylight hours or by any woman not charging by the hour.

Victoria's Secret comes along and suddenly husband buys you things to push up, pull up, and lace up all over again. They go through their second adolescence. However, adult son knows all about VS and any pink and white striped box or bag coming into the house is like a neon sign stating Dad's planning to get sex soon.

Just try throwing away the catalog when it comes in the mail. Those pages of models miraculously keep ending up in the bathroom. Who needs to pay for the *Sports Illustrated* Swim Suit Edition? The VS women are less clothed on every page and the catalog comes free right to the house.

I understand the whole male thing between innocent and naughty, but let's talk comfort. Give me a chenille peignoir or a size fourteen thong with Velcro. Make it simple, comfortable, and in normal sizes. No baby boomer worth her weight in salt is a size zero. Most of us were born a size ten and grew from there. Time to make flannel crotchless panties and comfortable alluring garments. Sexy comfort does not have to be an oxymoron, Victoria's Secret. The Baby Boomer generation may be moving out of the fast lane, yet we're still hot to trot towards our spouse.

Michael Jordan has commercials out for tag less underwear. No more scratching and itching in places you can't reach. What a minute. Guys can now buy their underwear tag-less because that little, itsy bitsy piece of starched ribbon bothers them? Yet we're supposed to wear miserable rash-creating lingerie? We keep ourselves from falling into depths of depression because we'll never look like Naomi Campbell in the Victoria Secrets commercials, while men get gorgeous Michael Jordan to bail them out of 100% cotton briefs with annoying tags.

Can we get a jury in here? Does anyone else see a problem with this picture?

The man invites umpteen people into my house.

He gets to fall into dead slumber after sex.

AND we're going to take the tags out of his soft, comfy cotton briefs?

I need another piece of chocolate.

This tells you where the next big wave in lingerie should be—The Comfort Zone. You can be sexy without having something tight and lacy cutting off your circulation.

Sex toys for CNS sufferers should be soft, uncomplicated, and quiet. An enclosed shower stall that fits two adults with a small seat for exhaustion is a perfect example.

Early morning and late at night can be awkward when living with your adult children. Slipping into something more comfortable for you may be a pair of fuzzy bunny slippers and an old comfortable sweater. You might be in for a surprise at what the Boomerangs wear around the house, though.

My advice is to buy them a new robe first thing. Nothing like staggering to the kitchen on a Saturday morning and finding your son with his head buried in the refrigerator and his backside covered with obscene dialogued boxers. It's not pretty.

Invariably, when you're expecting company, when your best friends from the office just walked through your front door, your son is waking up. He fumbles toward the shower in holey skivvies, bed hair sticking out in all directions. Robes must be mandatory and slippers optional in a crowded nest.

Threadbare outfits do not count as being completely dressed either.

I've seen more material on a Barbie outfit than what's left in some of the comfort suits our Boomerangs lounge around in. Yes, we raised them and changed their diapers decades ago. I don't want to see their tushies any more. Keep them covered and out of sight. I'm not a prude by any means, but do have a sensitive gag reflex.

I can't stress enough to respect yourself, and that means taking care of your body. You don't want them stronger than you when you have to wrestle for control of the remote. Include taking vitamins and eating right into your daily routine. Hiding a bag of miniature Hershey bars next to your bed is not the answer when dealing with adult children. Extra pounds will only make it more difficult to squeeze into the miniscule space they leave open for you on the couch.

I looked forward to getting a little older, becoming a woodland creature and being able to have more salad in my diet. Someone even invented the salad in a bag concept, pre-chopped lettuce and toppings, just for me. The kids would leave home and I could have salads for dinner—a Caesar one night, oriental chicken another night. Lettuce was an alien substance to my kids. Whether light-green iceberg lettuce or dark-green Romaine, they'd turn their noses up at anything looking like rabbit fodder. I found myself craving the cold green leaves and forced the kids to eat at Carl's Junior in the Eighties so I could gorge on the salad bar.

Salads and fresh fruits are expensive, I admit, yet important to combat the urge to gorge ourselves with eating anything in sight when adult children return home. Even quick and easy frozen dinners by Lean Cuisine and Weight Watchers are more and more expensive because the national corporations know they have you right where they want you, stressed and overweight. How can fewer calories in a box cost so much more? You can't afford to keep your calorie intake below 2,000 a day using the frozen boxed variety of menus when there are too many people living in your house . It's a Catch-22 in the kitchen.

Comfort food is a whole other matter. Do not let the Boomerangs stress you into eating your weight in frustration. Unfortunately, bulk carbohydrates are the cheapest food staples you can buy, and when your budget is breaking due to additional people at home, carbs are hard to ignore. Potatoes, noodles, and loaves of day old bread are cheap, easy fare when feeding masses, yet will add pounds to your waistline before you can say "Jack LaLane." Sauces are another great way to stretch out a pound or two of hamburger, yet the creamy base will glue itself to your hips. My mom was famous for fast and easy dinners after working all day. Her standard was browning a pound of hamburger, liberally seasoned with Lawry's, throwing in a can of corn or peas, then blending flour and milk with it for gravy. Pouring this skillet casserole over mashed potatoes was considered dinner. Quick, simple, and not a lot of arguing from anyone in the family because their mouths were full.

Stirring boiling pots of pasta with a tired arm after a long day at work, I wonder if my mom thought of one day cooking for two. I'm still waiting for that magical day; not holding my breath over it, but I refuse to give up hope. Making meals for short people again means we're back to carbo-loading. Pancakes for breakfast and peanut butter and jelly picnics for lunch. Dinner reeks of spaghetti or hot dogs, all the fattening foods that taste good, so you nibble your way into three extra sizes.

Nothing is more difficult than trying to stick to a sensible and healthy diet fare with Boomerangs in the house. It takes sweat-breaking endurance not to eat yourself through a bag of Hershey kisses when living in a crowded nest. You have so little you can do to make the world feel better, that the urge to keep a piece of chocolate tucked into your cheek is incredible. Stay strong. The body is not taking well to the strain of gravity pulling at the edges of my underarms and thighs.

Think portion control to help in the battle of the bulge. Think of using tiny tea set dishes instead of regular dishware. Buy a stack of four-ounce Pyrex cups to use for yourself. Use these for cereal or puddings, soups or stews. Want a piece of steak or other protein in your meal without gaining a half-pound? Use portion control and make sure it's the size of a deck of playing cards, not the complete works of Shakespeare. It's not always *what* you eat as it is *how much* you eat that makes a difference whether the bathroom scale will groan when you stand on it.

Use chopsticks instead of regular silverware to slow down your eating. Besides, it will give the grandchildren a good laugh. You can be the dinner theater entertainment. Try eating your food with an appetizer toothpick, one small piece at a time. Chew thoroughly, you know how we always harped on the children to chew their food. Slow down and take the same advice.

Chef Shaputis is not a moniker anyone will ever hear. I am a connoisseur of fine fast food dining. My delicate palette knows exactly what it wants on any given day from Quarter Pounders to Whoppers, extra value to super sized. If thousands of calories are forced into my system from the smorgasbords of chain restaurants my grandchildren drag me to, I demand quality ones.

I've a wild streak in the kitchen sometimes. Shh, don't tell anyone, I make my blue boxed macaroni and cheese without milk—I like it strong. I want the cheesiest flavor I can get. For a while our local grocery store sold blue canisters of the same powdered cheese and my oldest grandson and I poured mounds of extra flavor into our bowls of macaroni. If we could figure out how to just eat the powder without gluing our mouths closed, we would. Why they stopped selling this nectar of the palette is beyond my brain. What an ingenious condiment.

I live by the white and red labeled soda. Don't try to do a blindfold taste test on this Gramma, I can tell the difference between Diet Pepsi and Diet Coke. Breakfast, lunch, dinner and every five minutes in between, my hand is usually clutching a can, a twenty ounce plastic bottle, or a paper cup filled with delicious bubbly Diet Coke.

I married a man who likes the same soda-in-the-morning caffeine rush. A rare find, I realize. I do wish someone could invent a way to freeze dry Diet Coke so I could add the water at home. I'm building arms that resemble Popeye dragging in twelve-packs, twenty-four-packs, and plastic shopping bags of two-liter bottles of Diet Coke. It's a heavy addiction. And everyone in the family is mired in it.

I know, why am I drinking Diet Coke when I live in Starbuck territory? Coffee kiosks lurk in parking lots on every block as cute former Fotomat stations are now recreated into quality coffee-to-go drive-throughs. Sorry, Seattle, I want my caffeine carbonated. Give me a serve yourself soda bar, and I'm satisfied.

A high price tag on something edible does nothing for me. Smooth tasting Hershey's, euphoria dating back to childhood, is my passion—not Godiva—hands down. I live at our local Barnes & Noble part time and see tables of gold-boxed Godiva chocolate are stacked in perky piles. During holidays each box is tied with fancy color-coordinated ribbons and bows depending on the season. Expensive chocolate doesn't mean better—I broke down and tried Godiva once—wasn't impressed at all.

Who gave us the idea that expensive meant better? Because you bought it at Nordstrom instead of Target doesn't necessarily mean you got your money's worth. I have flattering yet comfortable clothes purchased from Target years and years ago that still receive compliments when I'm out and about. If it looks good, feels good, and is washable, I'm all for it.

The same goes with food and wine for me. One New Year's Eve, 1989, I thought how fun to celebrate with a bottle of champagne, a fancy dark-green bottle painted with decorative white flowers on the outside. The one you always see characters on television serving. A special touch to welcome in a new decade, and the last decade of the Twentieth Century. (No, don't get into the argument about exactly *when* a new decade or century starts. Just go with the story.)

Hubby and I went to a large liquor store in town and checked out the champagne section. California and French varieties filled shelf after shelf. The prices ran from low to chokingly high and right there sitting on the high priced side was my quest. Not only did they have a few bottles, but also a special gift box, satin lined, with four matching glasses included with the bottle of champagne. What a way to bring in the Nineties, and I walked out a lot poorer but excited with my purchase.

Midnight approached and hubby took the chilled bottle and popped the cork. He slowly poured the glasses, and as Dick Clark helped us ring in the new year, we kissed for luck, clinked our matching glasses together and took a sip.

Nothing.

Flavor, bite, carbonation—none of the above truly did it for me. My middle class palette didn't find anything to like with the famous champagne. Disappointment beat against my brain, but I stuck to "it's the thought that counts." I had chosen an adventure for this special occasion and was able to carry it through. I just like Asti Spumanti better.

Guess it's the same with chocolate for me. A frozen Mars or Three Musketeers bar on a warm summer evening is three shades of delight. Give me peanut M&M's or give me death. I'll fight you over a Hershey bar or arm wrestle you over a Reese Peanut Butter Cup. I'm a cheap date, what can I say?

I think I gained three pounds just talking about chocolate. Be serious about yourself and be moderate in eating. Remember our metabolism isn't as fast as it used to be as young women. Don't let CNS send you scarfing down whole bags of cookies or sweets. It's not worth the gazillion calories. What took a week or two to lose back when we were in college, now takes six months.

A killer for me is resisting the after-holiday sales of chocolate. You know the day after Halloween and Easter stores are unloading the same delicious bags of wrapped candy for 50% off, and you could stash a bag in your desk, one in the car, and another in your purse for minimal cost. Don't. What little enjoyment you'd get from the increase in brain chemicals will not cover the additional twenty pounds per holiday you'll gain in the process. Solid chocolate bunny ears go right to the inner thighs and stick there for eternity. Day after Christmas chocolate Santas head right for the butt and make themselves a permanent home. It's 50% off the cost now, but 200% agony later.

Learn to respect and take care of yourself. Your family won't. You can be creative in doing exercises. I find carrying the three-year-old grandson around is great for weight lifting. He's getting spoiled, I know, but I'm burning off a couple of calories. He's a solid thirty-six pounds. When I'm ambitious, I put him on my back and gallop a couple times around the outside of the house. You'd be amazed how I feel when I put him down. Getting this monkey off my back couldn't be easier.

However, moderation needs to be a factor, as jealousy will raise its ugly head. If I exercise by playing with one, I have to do something equally as physically draining with the other grandson. The eight-year-old will take you on in basketball and damage you if you're not careful. I bought a bike to go riding with him, but I draw the line at roller blades. No ramps or helmets for me, like I need flat hair AND a broken arm. Too big to carry, I will try lifting him once in a while for wrap around hugs. He misses being the baby and having more physical contact with Gramma.

He used to hold both my hands and pull himself over in a flip by walking up my thighs and shoving himself over. He could do this over and over if I let him. My arms got a good work out, but the back muscles sometimes screamed, "enough." Pony rides on the living room rug were popular for a long time, but now I resemble the song about the old gray mare. I ain't what I use to be.

The first couple years of CNS, I maintained my weight. Running additional errands, like picking up senior items and toddler shoes at opposite ends of Wal-Mart, kept additional calories from gaining ground.

I've suffered from CNS since 1993. Taking care of my mom provided a physical fitness benefit in a variety of ways. Things like lifting her into a wheelchair for a long walk through the neighborhood or a trip to the doctor, then lifting her back into her hospital bed, kept my arm muscles toned.

Jogging through drug stores to gather prescriptions (pharmacies are always in the back of the store) and notions probably added up to a couple of extra miles a week. You didn't feel strain in the short bursts and your metabolism stayed relatively high.

During that same first year of a crowded nest the oldest grandson was born, and I started to do a lot of things with the little guy glued to my hip. Those few extra pounds of baby helped whittle away calories here and there.

Then a funny thing happened, a piece of chocolate found its way to my mouth as a reward that I had done a decent day's work for many people. Who else was going to say thank you so deliciously? The baby took life for granted, and I was thanking my mom for hanging in as long as she did. Husbands don't say thank you, they say what do I get? Chocolate is quiet, goes down smooth with sweet ecstasy. I found myself gaining weight in leaping chunks and grams. Don't make the same mistake. Chocolate becomes a delicious, vicious mistress. She demands your money, your attention; she lulls you into a blood sugar depression craving more.

Just suck on carrot sticks and buy a case of chewing gum to keep yourself busy without gaining a pound here and there. Take care of yourself; no one else will. Do you see the mantra here? Sounds trite sometimes, but it's true. Pop those multi vitamins, build up your B vitamins, and beat the blues by being as healthy as you can. Get yourself over to GNC or your local health food store and pick up the timed-released women's vitamins with at least 75 mg of B's. The generic, poopy, grocery store shelf vitamins you throw in the basket at the last minute aren't going to cut the pressure and strain of being a CNS sufferer. You need good stuff, and it's worth the few extra bucks. Remember, look for "time released" on the label. The process let's your body absorb more of the B's to keep you going longer, keep you flowing along the maniacal list of errands and jobs ahead of you.

I started out, with my mom's maternal-baseball-bat-over-the-head encouragement, using Great Earth Vitamins and found by popping one multi tab at night before going to sleep, I could hit the floor when the alarm went off much easier and more alert. You gotta do whatcha gotta do to get through a crowded nest. B vitamins are a must. Throw in some vitamin C, too, while you're pill popping. You're worth it, trust me. And then you'll look great in that silk and chenille teddy when the day comes (if the day ever comes) that you and your husband can kick back and be romantic.

Interesting fact #347. Adult children hate to get their hands dirty. They won't bother you outside. Get yourself a copy of *Shovel It* by Eva Shaw—learn from the expert all the mental health and well-being bennies of gardening. Find out just how nurturing and healing this outdoor stuff can make you feel. Remember making mud pies as a child? Our first link to the therapeutic vibes of plunging our hands in moist, rich soil with the sun warming our backs started in our youth.

Sit under a tree, just about any kind of tree will do, and listen to nothing. No one asking for something, no laundry issues, no choosing your words carefully. Just you and a tree. If you don't have a front or back yard, create a window box garden of color and harmony to sit by.

I thought when I moved to the Northwest I had died and gone to Heaven. I now owned (or will after thirty years of payments to the bank) almost two acres of forest. I could walk in a rambling circle, along a dirt path under pines and mighty maples. Wild berry vines caught the edge of my pant legs with playful pleas for attention. Peace and solitude were all mine with no distracting neighbors behind us. I saw black tailed deer (distant relatives of *Bambi*?) and soft furry rabbits meander across the yard during the first few days after we moved in.

Then came the older son and his lowered cruise mobile with mufflers heard in the next state. The air shook and trembled as he worked on the engine or went out on a date. Grandsons discovered my path, playing bad guys, riding motor cross with their bikes up and down the trail. Neighbor children brought into my sanctuary were like short, loud blips of humanity staying for hours, using up the oxygen and ambiance.

Not content with additional bodies in the house, I added a chocolate labrador to the mix. Okay, he started out as a puppy, and I thought how cute an idea to get him as a present for hubby for Valentine's Day. You know, chocolate for Valentine's Day. I brought the puppy to his office in a basket wrapped in red cellophane as if it were chocolate for the whole department.

What a sap. Desperate for a romantic fix with a crowded household and nothing happening on my dance card for months, I fell for the old cute puppy trick. Puppy is now eighty-five pounds of jealous energy; leaping and bounding on legs made with coiled springs, he wants to sit on my lap just like the three-year-old.

He barks non-stop at anything moving in the backyard, be it branch or twig, cowering behind the patio table lest it be a deer or bear making the movements—bravado and cowardice all smushed into one gorgeous milk chocolate fur ball.

I saw my sweet, gentle deer one time after everyone moved in and the look on her face was pity. The eyes locked onto mine and as she slowly stepped away from our yard, I knew her life would continue on, minus the frustration and angst of mine. Her kids grew up and left, isn't that amazing? How'd she do that? If they tried to come back, she'll probably bite them hard in the back leg forcing them to flee. You know if I tried that, I'd be arrested for assault and battery, and I told you about the *Cops* show.

I'll curl up in my car safely parked on a deserted dirt road somewhere with the rain drenching the landscape and re-read my copy of *Shovel It*. Yes, Eva, it does make me feel better.

Be good to yourself as a CNS sufferer. Get plenty of rest wherever and whenever you can.

What was cute as young parents when dawn broke on the horizon and the kids ran in and jumped on the bed is now endured through clenched teeth as the grandchildren rush in on Saturday morning and do exactly the same thing. Is it a child thing, does someone give them a list of instructions at birth? Weekends are not for sleeping in again, as the grandsons run in to say the sun is up and everyone should be in the living room. It's like a fire drill. Worst alarm clock ever made, no snooze button, no gentle volume control. Just boom, slamming the bedroom door open first thing every Saturday and Sunday. He's only three, and swears he can't tell the days of the week, yet I guarantee you he will sleep until 9 a.m. Monday through Friday when he has preschool. How do they know?

Whining about the lack of privacy in our bedroom to other adults usually brings the same response—put a lock on the bedroom door. Actually there is one of those push button locks in the doorknob of my bedroom from the previous owner of the house. However, it's worn and only provides a split second or two more warning time when you turn the knob before opening.

I've thought about replacing it, and I wouldn't miss the blasts of pre school enthusiasm before the break of dawn demanding I get up. I just know that instead the wake up call would be a merciless pounding on the door, and incessant twisting of the knob. A lock doesn't mean I'd actually get to sleep in on a Saturday morning. It's just a different alarm clock. I'd still have a no win situation and I'm not thrilled about starting my day to the beat of a pounding door.

Hey, I was dreaming of being alone with Richard Gere handing me a sinful-looking basket of chocolate or something warm and sweet, when I hear the call "Sun's on, Gramma. Get up!" Not like anything was probably going to happen anyway. Might as well get up and watch a few hours of Power Rangers. Maybe they'll re-run an episode starring Tommy of the Mighty Morphin Power Rangers for Gramma being such a good sport.

6

Which Sandwich Are You?

Classic literature and a few old black and white movies tell us families shared overcrowded domiciles as an economic necessity for hundreds of years. Aunts and uncles lived in back rooms; grandma and grandpa were always there when you came home from school. The whole neighborhood around you shared in similar situations. Multi-generational families have lived together since the Pilgrims landed.

Sometime after World War II people started moving into single-family dwellings. You left the old neighborhood and went out into the world to set up housekeeping in a cracker-boxed-sized tract house. Just mom, dad, and the kids. Total square footage of a house went into four digits. People stretched out, the recliner was invented, larger couches, king sized beds. A new generation grew up thinking it was the norm for family members to live, not just in different rooms of the same house, but in different time zones.

Automobiles and telephones made keeping in touch easier. You wanted to know how Pop's doing, you picked up the phone. You piled in the car for cross-country vacations to meet and greet new additions and aging family members once or twice a year.

Nothing changes but the changes; everything old is new again. Choose a cliché. Whatever it was called back then when families lived together it was still crowded and it seems to be back in vogue.

Label, label, label—our generation gets more labels than its fair share; not only are we baby boomers, but many of us also fall into the label of the Sandwich Generation. Being a member of the sandwich generation means being caught in the carnival ride of: (1) what our *children* need and want; (2) what *we* need and want; and (3) what our *aging parents* need and want.

An estimated twenty-two percent of the American population can be classified within the Sandwich Generation by definition. Some estimates, made by those invisible powers that make up statistics and numbers we ooh and aah over on the evening news, show nearly two-thirds of the baby boomer generation will be taking care of an elderly parent in the next decade.

In 1990, before the Crowded Nest Syndrome took the lead headlines from the Empty Nesters, *Newsweek* reported the average woman (well, none of us reading this book is average, so that leaves us out) spends approximately seventeen years raising children and eighteen years helping aging parents. The Sandwich Generation, living with young or adult children and maybe grandchildren at home, while handling the needs of aging parents, creates the perilous loss of ability to plan for our own dreams and goals. This stress can lead some people to the edge.

I've come up with assorted deli sandwich names for different possible lifestyles of the membership. I told you we are the generation of labels. Which one do you resemble?

Baby Boomer Beef, Hold the Mayo: You have more in your house besides your spouse, with daily outside responsibilities to your aging parents, running errands, possibly taxiing them to appointments now and again. They haven't actually moved in with you yet.

The Works: Aging parent(s), adult children, and grandchildren living with you. An ultimate multi-generational crowded nest concept.

Pastrami with Onions: The stress of juggling schedules, workload, and relatives gives you heartburn and gas.

Peanut butter and jelly: The lower middle class tax level, too little income to afford anything, money going out in all directions, financial hardships along with the responsibilities.

Vegetarian Delight: The balanced diet, something light and easy. You baby-sit the grandkids or carpool them; you do the grocery shopping for the aging parents but you get to come home to a place of peace and quiet in between.

Some baby boomers, who will remain nameless to protect the guilty, raised children back in the Seventies, divorced in the Eighties, remarried in the Nineties, and started a new family. What were you thinking? Didn't you have enough book reports and smelly gym clothes; you wanted to go through raising a child again? You looked across your lattes into your new spouse's face and said, "yes, let's have a baby together." Can science have your brain for research when you die? You *chose* to give up peaceful Saturday mornings for the next umpteen years to satisfy some biological clock on purpose, incredible. Add to that household the possibility of an aging parent in the very near future. Diapers and Geritol.

My view is different from most baby boomers' perspective of multi-generational cohabitation. Been there, done that. I lost a huge block of prime time television shows during years of having three generations in one house. Either I watched mind-numbing Barney videos over and over with a toddler or twenty-four-hour-a-day news broadcasts with a bed-ridden mother, including quizzes over the day's headlines mandatory afterwards. My brain became a bowl of saccharin-sweet oatmeal with razor-sharp nails embedded in it.

It's one thing to turn forty. Hallmark makes fun of the rite of passage and party stores everywhere carry Over the Hill decorations. You might dread it, you worry about it, the gray hairs start showing and you know the fast lane of life has merged into the middle lane. It's another thing to have your whole life turned upside down at forty.

A nasty case of bronchitis took me down a week before my fortieth birthday. Exhausted from minimal oxygen and hacking up gallons of mucus, all celebrations were cancelled. Was this an omen of the year ahead, the decade ahead? I was too sick to care—then.

Months of my own pre-planning party preparations were shot to hell. Hey, I know my group. If I want special things to happen for me, I take the initiative and get them going with details and loose ends. December 3rd was supposed to be spent on a luxurious cruise ship heading out towards the warm, sunny Caribbean. I plunked a healthy deposit down on this dream vacation back in July.

I didn't dread turning forty, just the opposite. I wanted to celebrate this milestone in style. I couldn't wait to be forty, with thoughts of other successful over-forty women to imitate. Sally Fields, Goldie Hawn, Jane Seymour, and many more of the women I'd watched on big screens and television, turned forty and looked happier than ever.

I booked hubby and I on a Big Red Boat to be pampered and fed on the high seas with a few Disney characters thrown in to keep me young. Remember I was born and raised in southern California. Disneyland was like going to Uncle Walt's house a couple of times a year. I earned this vacation after a tumultuous decade of my thirties, I wanted to party into a new era, establish a foundation of fun and frolic for my forties.

Silly me. First indication of a disastrous storm ahead was that hubby's back went out, with crippling pain, in mid-October, over something trivial like pulling up his sock. Week after week of being off work and enduring his HMO's frequent physical therapy sessions did nothing to relieve the pain. By November we knew if he was ever going to stand upright again, he needed major back surgery.

Remember the dawn of the 1990's found us all at the mercy of dreaded HMO's? New hybrid health insurance organizations leaching power and decisions right out of your doctor's hands, leaving you suffering through mounds of paperwork to plead your pain to a committee of accountants. These groups of patronizing baboons carelessly denied claims of thousands of average patients every day. My husband's blown back meant nothing to them.

We'd probably still be waiting for a referral if husband's employer hadn't picked up the phone and demanded the HMO do something to fix their employee and return him to his job immediately or they'd find another insurer. A surgical date popped up on the horizon.

We won the battle for surgery, but I lost my birthday trip. The travel agent sympathized with me as she canceled our reservations. My magical fortieth celebration on the high seas was gone. Fortunately, I'm not a bitter person. Yet.

For hubby's fortieth, I schemed and planned an entire year in advance to throw him a Parrothead surprise party. Parrotheads are die hard Jimmy Buffett fans, and hubby lived and breathed in three-quarter time. Decorations of papier-mâché shark fins and colorful, hand-painted posters were created and stored at work. I even managed to get Jimmy Buffet to autograph one of his books with "Happy Birthday" for the birthday boy, as friends, family, and neighbors joined me in making it a great memory. I probably had more fun putting the festive event together than the guest of honor had attending it, so I'm not holding a grudge that he entered his forties with a big shebang and I got a dud.

In all fairness, even in back pain Hubby worked with one of my girlfriends to throw a surprise get together of my co-workers and friends during a happy hour. He got the surprise, however, when I couldn't imagine getting out of bed on the appointed day, let alone drive anywhere with croupy bronchitis robbing me of oxygen, life force, and the will to open my eyes.

(Note to all: a dual surprise celebration with some dear friends whose husband's birthday was close to mine did manage to take place. I wasn't totally bereft of salutations. I didn't want strains of violin music and snow appearing outside the window while you're reading this.)

Are you making a list of the negative crises adding up during this point in my life? I'm not done. My mother's health, never great over the previous twenty years battling a crippled back and COPD (chronic obstructive pulmonary disease), dramatically declined that year. It took a nose dive into "oh, my gawd, this could be it." Long discussions among my siblings and nieces of possible nursing homes ripped our family's hearts.

Before my birthday we knew she needed surgery and expected a difficult recovery period. This wonder woman matriarch of the family had lived her whole life under the yokes of working full time to put food on the table, sacrificing, scrimping while micro managing the trials and tribulations of her offspring. Being the youngest with a healthy canyon of years between my siblings and me, I saw only a pittance of what this woman could do and had done for countless people. I idolized her as a child. Her strength and rock-fast determination to prevail for good were my role models.

To find her stripped of everything she cherished most—independence, the ability to drive, and worst of all the pleasure of giving everyone else simple pleasures from her almost daily shopaholic treks—I picked up the baton to be the family glue. The decision to move her into our house took some persuasion to convince my mom it was the best thing to do. By now you realize hubby has this big ol' soft heart about inviting people to live with us.

We turned our front room with cathedral ceilings into a studio apartment for her. Medicare rental suppliers sent over a hospital bed, portable oxygen equipment, and a machine for breathing treatments. We set the bed up against the large front window, her television and VCR sat at the foot of the bed (thank goodness for remote controls), and she was ready for visitors to keep her company.

Adult daughter, single and actually living away from home, moved back to help take care of her grandmother during the day while I was at work. Not that we pleaded with her to give up a high paying career or her last year of college to make this sacrifice. Did I mention she was pregnant?

Happy birthday, welcome to forty. Three generations, soon to be four, living under one roof right at the pinnacle of my life.

The year quickly dropped straight down from there. Medals of dedication and valor under fire could have been given out during those next six months. A crowded nest demands creativity and inventiveness to survive the closeness of many adult relations under one roof. Add to that mix the Richter scale mood swings of a pregnant adult child as well as an aged matriarch fighting her own tsunami's of depression finding herself bed bound. You walked through my front door at your own risk. Alone together Monday through Thursday during daylight working hours was a long dangerous stretch for grandmother and granddaughter. Too much alike, both head strong, both going through extreme opposite ends of the emotional scale, some days I didn't know what I might find when I came home from work.

Opening the front door, the greeting was two blaring televisions at maximum volume. Before I could put my purse down, one or both started vying for attention and a fresh ear to bend over their sufferings of enduring the other. Include in this welcoming committee two older ninety-pound yellow labs meeting me at the door. Thank goodness they couldn't talk, or I'd have had to listen to their versions of the house bound women's adventures as well.

Surviving the stress and strain of a crowded nest takes patience, lots of deep breathing to maintain a high level of oxygen, and Prozac. The miracle yellow and green pill should be passed out to every human being. Heck, add it to the water supply and make it easier on the world. No crowded nest dwelling should be without a medicine cabinet filled with a decent sized prescription of these happy drugs. Dealing with continued major stress day after day without Prozac is like trying to build a house without a hammer. Not that it couldn't be done, but why would you want to?

The year I turned forty and found myself working full time supporting three generations in my house was the year I discovered the calming properties of Prozac. Some day I'd like to meet the inventor of Prozac, and give him or her a big hug. My hero, who's recipe or formula resulted in a phenomenal product giving me endurance to keep putting out when the world adds more and more to my plate.

If my life is a test of the emergency broadcasting system of mental health, Prozac is the safety whistle. You take aspirin for a headache. You take Prozac for CNS. Take a couple of aspirin or Tylenol, too. The body will ache from the weight of supporting all these people.

The first grandchild arrived, and if I wasn't putting my elbow into a plastic tub by the kitchen sink to wash the baby, I was giving my mom a shot of pain medication to help relieve her symptoms. My daughter ran up and down the stairs of the house and my nerves in between the world's of her grandmother's and a little infant's needs.

Don't fall into the trap of reverting to being a child when your parent or parents move in with you. Issues of childhood, the feeling of neglect or abandonment, the pony you never got from Santa or the beating with a belt for something no one remembers, can't be dragged out of the closet and hammered over their heads. You're a grown up; don't forget it. Let go of the past heartaches; don't whine and threaten over them. That doesn't mean you can't sit down over a cup of coffee some time and ask about the past.

In fact, I urge you to use whatever bits and pieces of time you can scrounge up to sit with them and ask questions about their youth as well as your own. Go ahead and ask calmly and conversationally why you didn't get a pony for your seventh birthday. You may find out that your parents were facing horrendous financial demons and did the best they could for you with what they had at the time. Or a horse kicked your dad when he was growing up, and he can't stand to be around them anymore.

Survival in a household of multi-generations is found in getting them all to talk to one another, not just to you. Get them to ask questions of each other so they'll provide their own entertainment. Let grandma tell your children about growing up in different times. Let your adult children explain the Internet to your parents. Get a book on writing memoirs and use the questions to spark monologues. The treasures revealed will be worth the time and effort. Write your own memoirs, I am. I'm calling it *A Princess Looks at 50,* available in paperback in early 2004. Sandwiches are made out of layered tastes in one bite. Tell your story and get down your parents' story.

Then go out to www.GorhamPrinting.com and find out how to publish those invaluable stories into a book.

My older brother came to live with us three months after my mom passed away. He needed a place to stay while rearranging his life and waiting out the long qualification process for disability. He didn't have the money to support himself while waiting to jump through the bureaucratic hoops. The fact that most days he couldn't breathe, and we could reach 911 just by hitting redial on our phone, didn't seem to move the paperwork any faster. Brother's favorite band is the Grateful Dead and there were times I wondered if he wasn't going to join them, literally.

Adult daughter still lived upstairs with eight-month-old grandson. So we had a daughter, a small but mobile grandson, and a fifty-something brother whose health was bordering on flat line. Don't forget the two yellow slugs, uh, dogs. Welcome to my world.

The two relative boarders, of course, didn't get along. The grandson was a great band-aid for most of the tension. I ran to work every morning and tried not to worry about who would be alive when I got home. I solved one concern by putting the baby in a Montessori school during the day. He was in a fun place, and daughter went back to school toward a new career in the travel industry. Brother's health stabilized, and he's blooming in northern California's fresh air.

My crowded nest began back in the early Nineties and hasn't stopped since. The occupants may have changed a time or two, encouraged by my husband's revolving door policy, but the house is never empty. Noisy, never quiet. Cluttered, never clean.

I wanted my dad to come live with me here in the great Pacific Northwest. During the last couple of years he seems to be in overtime in the game of life, but he won't discuss moving in. Do you blame him? Too many people under my roof already, where would another person fit? How many more corners do we have to fill? So at this point, I don't have to worry too much about being a card-carrying member of the sandwich generation, cuz my surviving parent flatly says no to the hospitality. I don't blame him for not wanting to move in; this isn't my favorite place either. Maybe I could move in with him.

Short people, tall people, young and old have lived and currently live in my house. My sister calls this place "Hotel Shaputis." Speaking of hotels, remember I talked about this in the last chapter, getting away for a weekend once a year or so for me is a major financial and logistic endeavor. However, walking into a hotel room brings tears to my eyes. The blessed silence, the made bed and dusted furniture are nirvana to my soul. I fall on my knees and kiss the carpet in reverence.

The sandwich generation isn't unique in the whole scheme of things we call life. It's been done in most of the generations in our country. Just a few differences this time around. Your life seems more taxing, yet you don't have to go out in the backyard to kill and clean a chicken for dinner. Your budget may include Pampers as well as Depends, but you don't have to wash your family's mountain of dirty clothes on an old scrub board in a wooden tub. Take the pleasures where you can get them.

Everything old is new again, as more and more aging parents are moving in with their children. We got out of the mode of enduring multi levels of people, needs, and wants under the same roof. It takes a little getting used to. A few more Excedrin days, a little more ball juggling, and higher utility bills.

You get sympathy from other friends and total strangers going through the same situation. It's amazing how our parents all start to fall apart about the same time. We lean on one another, share stories about getting through each day, trying to make them a little easier.

Don't ever say, "It could be worse," and tempt Fate to make it so, because it will. Fate has a sick sense of humor. Just find the benefits and memories in the corners of the clutter and noise and stick them in your ears for some peace and quiet relief.

Why do people, i.e. relatives, want to live at my house? Anyone needing to do a research paper on the Crowded Nest Syndrome please contact me. One interesting section is on the attitudes of the post-parental units.

I am not the greatest, easiest, fill-in-a-descriptive-word-here, person to live with.

Let me give you some examples. I'm broke most of the time, and broke people are usually crabby people. Not the Walton's mountain folk where having no money means more room for bigger hearts. I mean the working-class, deep in debt crabby. Well, okay, I tend to forget I have no money and pull out the plastic. I see my family's enjoyment or satisfied security in my financial senility. They've all learned to take advantage of the fact that the brain cells assigned to me when I can't afford something are not functioning.

The three-year-old has learned about infomercials from getting up in the middle of the night and plunking himself in front of the television. He's yanked on my covers to tell me I need the new pasta pans that lock and load for easy cook and drain procedures. I can't remember if he liked the white one better than the red one. He can count to twenty-two and read now, which means he's starting to memorize 1-800 numbers. Grownups can buy these things, it says so right on the television. You have to be over eighteen to call now, and big brother tells him my exact age often. It's larger than twenty, so I'm eligible.

And if a short person watching infomercials wasn't bad enough, the oldest grandchild has learned you can buy things from the Internet. Third grade students get touch typing instruction, so at the lightning speed of twenty words a minute he keeps filling out these onscreen forms with buying information like our shipping address and waits for me to come home and fill in the credit card information. Wrong. Thank you publicly funded elementary school. First you teach him how to read the banner ads, and now touch typing helps him fly through the forms.

Another good reason not to live at my house, I snore. Not lady-like slumber noises, we're talking the rumble of a Southern Pacific train going through the house. This doesn't stop people from moving in, though, no matter how often I wake them up. I am not going to spend money I don't have on the latest wonder devices or medical procedures for snoring. I've woken up the three-year-old sleeping in the next room. All right, and the dog, and probably the neighbors if I have a cold. You can't say I do it on purpose, because no one moves out from it.

Why is my house filled with other people?

7

Happy Holiday Horrors

Breaking the shrink-wrap on a brand-new calendar gives me a brief glimmer of hope the new year is going to be different. I am never disappointed. Me have a dull year? What's that? I don't pray for happiness, chant with worry beads toward the east, or click my ruby-slippered heels together three times for success. Nor do I wish each page of the new calendar brought with it peace and quiet—why work myself into a miserable snit? Ain't gonna happen; wouldn't be prudent. Sorry, Dana Carvey, I can't do justice to your impersonation of the first President Bush. But you know what I mean.

Speaking of Presidents, who's in charge of creating holidays? We need a National CNS Day. Anybody know the number to the White House? How about a national conference centered around a holiday for CNS where at least once a year thousands of post-parental units gather in a weekend of recharging dead batteries, remembering how to smile and enjoy themselves?

One night will be reserved for a superbly prepared dinner with cloth napkins, crystal glasses, and soft, comfortable high back chairs. Racks of evening gowns and cocktail dresses that haven't been borrowed and stained by their adult children will be available for the women to choose from. Revlon would donate cartons of foundation, blush, eye shadows in various flattering shades and moisturizing lipsticks for revitalizing the beauty strained by Crowded Nest Syndrome.

Every attendee would receive a free goody bag filled with pampering amenities such as a soft cushy bathrobe and matching slippers to use during the spa treatments. Hour long massages and facials would be available day or night. A separate meeting room would be converted into a movie theater showing non-stop comedy films, because we all know the benefit of laughter.

Imagine, a holiday just for those of us supporting the extra weight of familial members. Our cute cartoon icon would be the infamous clutter fairy, swooping into our lives with a gigantic magic wand to produce abundant floor space and organization out of chaos. Space saver gadgets would fill department store shelves with banners and posters encouraging friends to buy and give to CNS sufferers everywhere. Bright colored greeting cards wishing mental and emotional health in humorous slogans and poems would appear months before the actual CNS holiday. Hallmark and American Greetings would compete for the highest sales figures.

Yes, that would do. (I've gone online and filled out the paperwork to make June 12th National CNS Awareness Day. Y'all look for a line of greeting cards and paper goods to be out in the next few years.)

I hate cooking. I'm not a bad cook, but I'm not a great cook. I know how to read a recipe and whip up some concoction from a page out of *Family Circle* magazine. I do okay around pots and pans with a wooden spoon. I can find my way in and out of a pantry without getting claustrophobia. It just seems like I've spent over a fourth of my life in a kitchen making breakfast, lunch, and dinner for people. Cooking is not my idea of a great time. And invariably I go to make a pan of fudge to tide myself over during Christmas panic attacks, and I'm missing one lousy ingredient. And half the time, since I'm in dire straits and have to have it now, my trip to the grocery store in bedroom slippers and baggy paint-stained sweatshirt will mean they are out of that one particular item.

During annual holidays everyone in my immediate family expects marvelous things to come out of the kitchen. Mainly they want past culinary delights re-created for their drooling pleasure. Hold the shouting and arguing, please. Remember, I'm not from Julia Child's gene pool. Holiday fares are simple and fattening. I can guarantee grease, sugar, and lethargy afterwards.

Thanksgiving means a couple boxes of Mrs. Culbertson's dressing with maximized chopped celery and minimized chopped onion. A liberal sprinkling of Lawry's seasoning salt on the turkey before roasting is a must. Nothing fancy, nothing exotic, just tummy warming food that has been on the table year after year. No oysters in the stuffing or candied cauliflower. Ocean Spray cranberry sauce, three cans minimum, and maybe the traditional green bean casserole if someone feels ambitious.

Christmas dinner, then, is usually ham and potato salad. My mom's recipe for the potato salad includes dill pickles and a touch of yellow mustard. Again, simple, yet it can make your mouth water at the strangest times. Jazz up any major holiday meal with a few cans of Graber's Olives out of Ontario, California, and adult children, relatives, and complete strangers are guaranteed to show up at the table.

So for what little I do in the kitchen to create full course meals for the holidays, the family puts up with my renditions of the same menu year after year. Hey, the holidays only come once a year. If they want to eat, they take what they get. If anyone else wants to take over the duties, by all means; I'll relinquish my apron. Uh, I don't have an apron, make it the potholders.

If not invited to someone else's party or bash, Super Bowl Sunday means a variety of dips to last the day and possibly into Monday evening arm chair quarterbacking over the highlights with leftovers. The menu always includes seven-layer dip, a baked ham and cheese concoction, and piles of finger foods. Knives and forks are outlawed during the game. Stress and tension during critical plays are not the place for weapons. And that includes going for the last Wahini weenie during a time out.

It's a Catch-22 situation. You want to enjoy the last tailgate party style game of the season, but setting out food and drinks guarantees the RAC's and other family members will be right there gobbling major quantities before you can fill your plate. Try begging for an invitation to someone else's affair whenever you can. They may not lay out a great spread, but you don't have to fight off other people for every mouthful, either.

At our house football is important; not just Super Bowl, though we don't watch every college bowl game any more. Too many super sized events scheduled over three days leaves us celebrating some of the originals, the Rose Bowl, the Orange Bowl, and maybe the Sugar Bowl. Or which-ever game USC is playing in that year.

During her high school years adult daughter was a Florida State fan and that got testy during a few seasons of my being married to an official USC alumni football player. I try to stay fairly neutral during football sea-son. The grandsons are too young yet to be waiting for The Call, and Gramma wants to be flexible to root for whatever college picks them up.

Holidays in general are challenging in a crowded nest. Make arrange-ments way ahead of time, it helps fake out the rest of them. I hide the piles of decorations or gifts out of sight of any suspecting relative—because all it takes is one wrong placement of a package of party supplies and Fate will step in to ensure the whole deal is off.

The aura of the birthday fairy for Boomerangs is right up there with Freddie Krueger. At least when adult children aren't living under foot, you can mail off a card with some money and hope they enjoy themselves. Quick, easy, and the postal service handles the worst of it.

When you have adult children under your roof and their date of birth rolls around, the expectations triple while visions of Visa and MasterCard dance through their heads. They remember Mom doing all the big and best stuff to celebrate milestones of turning eight, twelve, even sixteen. Where are the clowns and magicians for their party? Where's the mom who invited the whole class for pizza and games every year? In debt, that's where.

Ever see a twenty-something pout because you didn't remember double chocolate cake with banana filling was their favorite? It's pitiful. I'm supposed to kick in for dinner out, with an expensive gooey dessert, plus a gift. It's more and more and more. Unlimited long distance phone cards are a staple and something with four-wheel drive and a CD player would be appreciated.

Getting them underwear for a present really pisses them off—I love it. It's the little things as a post-parent you look for and grab when you can. Giving them underwear twice in a row, though, doesn't work. Then you're just being mean and spiteful. Do it to them on every other occasion or gift wrap a pair of fancy socks. You gotta love the little things.

Grownups have no business watching Saturday morning cartoons, yet there's a twenty-four-hour-a-day cable show called Cartoon Network that plays Boomerang cartoons, dating back from the mid-Sixties to early Eighties. They know there are adult children and grandparents up at the crack of dawn with jammie-clad munchkins.

If you stay awake after the Boomerang shows until a more civilized hour of the morning, the various generations of Power Rangers come on. From the original Mighty Morphins each group thereafter has evolved to Turbo-sized, in Space, Time warped, Wild Forcing, Ninja Storm young whipper snappers in one piece body suits. Flash backs of Tommy once in a while are my favorites. I had Superman in black and white splendor; my grandkids get hypnotized by primary colored spandex heroes.

Three hundred times an hour during these bad animation or karate-styled do-gooder shows, there are toy commercials. During the months before Christmas, why bother putting a cartoon in between the commercials, just move the talking giraffe into my house and be done with it. Someone call my investment broker and check on how much stock I have in the pink bunny's company. I'd double it, but I need the extra money to buy more batteries. Christmas is ho ho ho how much is it going to cost me?

When the oldest grandson was about three, we started a routine during the endless onslaught of toy commercials. He'd perked up during a plastic action figure advertisement and say, "I want that." Hubby's quick response was "put it on your list." Let Santa take the responsibility of the mass bombardment of possibilities and disappointments. Two seconds later, another commercial of sweet smiling kids playing a to-die-for game of chance comes on. I'd hear the echo of "I want that"—"Put it on your list."

Fast forward five years, and here comes the second three-year-old living with us, and we spend a whole pre-Christmas weekend hearing "I want" "I want" out of him and hubby doesn't lift his head from the newspaper but says "Put it on the list." No one noticed the look on the boy's face as the same audio scenario played on and on.

Finally this short tyrant puts his fists on both hips and yells, "What list?"

Who forgot to explain to the new kid about writing a letter to Santa Claus? You'd think in a crowded nest everyone would know everything about everything.

Christmas used to mean suffering through blistering frustration with strands of tangled lights for the tree and fighting with the husband to put lights on the house. Why should he? All of our kids were teenagers and wouldn't even be home much during the month of December. Sounded like sweat and smashed thumbs for nothing.

We switched to an artificial tree in a box, and I didn't get too carried away with decorating much more than that, because no one appreciated the energy or efforts. They wanted the money to go toward their gifts. The day was coming soon when the house would be empty of kids, and we could spend Christmas's catching a plane to Cabo or Hawaii, maybe even a train to Canada. Just away, travel reservations would be our gifts. Never happened, probably never will.

The Boomerangs moved back with grandkids and Christmas decorating went into hyper drive. We have lighted reindeers in the front yard, a mommy and a fawn. White icicle-styled lights outline the roof on the front of the house. And a huge tree, still artificial but pre-lit with fifteen hundred white lights, is set up the day after Thanksgiving for maximum holiday exposure.

Though we are back to hiding the presents again, and learning the difference between Pokemon and Digimon, at least one thing is easier this time around with grandchildren. Where before there was the Sears catalog for the kids to scribble and circle their favorite toys, now there's the Internet and half a dozen places the grandkids can write up their list of wants. Doing the shopping online does ease some holiday headaches.

Befriend the Internet and make it do your work for you. I'd buy it something special for all its help, but it's happy if I just show up. If I hit the mute button on the machine, I can sit in quiet while I shop. Well, if I go online in the middle of the night and no one hears the click of the on button. I like to go to Claus.com and play with the elves. Sick little twerps.

Nothing is more frustrating to a grandparent than trying to put together the umpteenth tricycle during the wee hours of Christmas with a bad back and sore knee. Pay the extra money to have Toys R Us do the bolts and screws. And Christmas again starts at 4:30 in the morning with the little munchkins running in and jumping in the middle of the bed. Broken ribs and heart palpitations, doesn't everyone start out Christmas this way?

Do grandchildren realize Santa needs time to travel around the world and get back to the North Pole before they start ripping and tearing into the gifts? No patience. That's the problem with the newer generations. Well, their parents were the same way, but we were twenty or thirty years younger, too.

Christmas afternoon all I want from Santa is a nap. A long warm snuggly nap. Instead I'm outside with the video camera watching new bikes and roller blades being test driven for the first time. Or clanging pans together in the kitchen because the adult kids want the same "memories" of Christmas meals as their own childhoods. Sure, I have nothing better to do, and you know how much I love being in the kitchen.

Before you get a chance to recover from Jingle Bells and Sugar Plum Fairies, here comes New Year's Eve. There's nothing more romantic on my calendar then a candlelight dinner and dancing, singing Auld Lange Syne at midnight with strangers, enhanced with a special good luck kiss. Now New Years is more about wiping chocolate fingerprints off your face instead of eye shadow, and jelly kisses instead of lipstick. Makeup never had so many calories.

Grandsons have no problem staying up to watch the ball drop in New York. I want to watch my eyelids drop at 9 p.m. my time which is midnight in New York, doesn't that count? I know in my heart Dick Clark is doing his job up on an icy rooftop with the countdown, I don't have to see the crowds of people standing in Times Square to know they're there. The grandchildren don't believe me. Huh, they probably don't believe in the Clutter Fairy either, but you and I know she's alive and avoiding my house.

I don't want to start off a new calendar year with sleep deprivation. For the next 364 days, I'm struggling to play catch up. Does champagne make kids sleepy? Too bad, we'll never know. Is there a Tylenol PM made for little people? Can someone make something up that takes the charge out of their batteries to let them sleep? Somebody's missing a big cash boat here!

The meds could be used for 21st Century children wound up tight worrying about the world before bedtime. They're concerned about learning the middle of the alphabet, why "7 ate 9," and how Clifford grew so big when he was the runt of the litter. I don't remember my adult children having such deep stress lines in their foreheads when they were little.

Halloween is back in full swing at my house with grandsons on board. This year I got costumes ahead of time off the Internet for the two boys so they'd have a chance to wear them and play in them to get more enjoyment than just the one night routine. I bought three mega-jumbo bags of wrapped candy from Costco, but all three disappeared before Columbus Day. The adult kids gobble them down by the handful each night. Isn't that amazing. I go through fifty dollars worth of candy during Halloween, and none of it ever makes it into a trick or treat bag. Scary, isn't it? I don't have to wear a costume when I answer the front door; the fright lines on my face and gray hair are enough to scare the local children into hysteria.

In CNS homes, chocolate is treasured and hoarded like gold.

Another calorie intense holiday is Valentine's Day. Visions of little paper cards shaped like Scooby Doo and NASCAR drivers dance in my pockets, the floor of the car and in couch cushions for weeks after the school parties are over. I've thought about writing a reverse ransom note with those candy conversation hearts, "Will pay to be kidnapped." What are those things made of anyway? They last forever at the bottom of my purse. When was the last time V-Day meant anything romantic around your house? Cupid has a hard time making an appearance in a crowded nest with too many moving targets.

Easter in my childhood meant the kitchen smelled like cider vinegar. Those ancient times when boiling hot water and two tablespoons of vinegar were needed to dissolve the colored egg dye in ceramic coffee cups. What did children use for coloring eggs whose parents didn't drink coffee? Oh, right that was in the 1950's and parents weren't allowed NOT to drink coffee. The parent police mandated it.

Now egg dyes come in plastic squeezable packets, liquid and ready to add to cold water. No vinegar, no scalding hot water to freak out parents when a normally clumsy child who spills a glass of milk regularly at meal times is supposed to suddenly become able to maneuver around hot steaming cups of colored water for the duration of the ceremony in coloring eggs. Only a man could dream up that combination for disaster.

It does take some of the nostalgia out of the holiday. You have plastic buckets with spinning gears to swirl the egg through paint, or stickers, or marking pens. All safe, non-toxic, and usually washable. Meaning if the egg gets wet after it's colored, it turns back into a plain, old hard boiled egg and you can throw the kiddies into the bath tub and find their natural tones under the pinks and greens of egg dye.

It's childhood traditions rearing its ancient head back in your home when you're a fulltime grandparent. If you think as a post-parental unit you're going to get out of eating three pounds of egg salad sandwiches for a week after Easter, you're sadly mistaken. The good news is you can buy bags of chocolate eggs and not have to worry about the store clerk raising an eyebrow. They don't have to know it's all for you. Well, that's the plan as you walk out the automatic door with the shopping cart. You'll find nothing but empty candy wrappers if you don't hide it well and the Boomerangs find them first.

A solid one-pound chocolate bunny is nirvana in the freezer as a chew toy for CNS sufferers. Be practical, hide it inside an empty frozen peas bag. It's something to gnaw on in frustration to wear out those jaw muscles when you can't whine and attack the adult children. And for a fat-free treat because you deserve it when the Easter bunny comes knocking, there are Peeps. The one and only incredible Peeps, the official artificial comfort food.

Celebrating a new century Peeps have taken a dramatic leap forward in merchandizing and commercialism. You can find Halloween Peeps in ghosts and black cats. Thanksgiving has orange pumpkin-shaped Peeps. Christmas brings us white snowmen in the traditional Peeps cellophane box. Share the official baby boomer dream food with your family.

What was the first candy to cross over into all holidays? M&M's! No more tediously picking out just the red and green ones out of various sacks for your winter holiday candy dish and then finding out they stopped making the red ones for some trumped up reason like the dye was bad for us. Who was going to eat three million red M&M's to see if that particular dye caused cancer? Thank goodness science, politics or people pressure prevailed and put that insanity behind us. Do you remember where you were in the mid-Eighties when they brought the red ones back?

Now you can purchase those bite-sized chocolate morsels in red, white, and blue for the 4th of July, earth tones for Thanksgiving, and even speckled pastel colored ones for Easter. Mix and match peanut M&M's and Crispy for added variety to each holiday.

Birthdays, Christmas, and other assorted days on the calendar (like Thursdays, or Sundays) are great times to hide out in the bedroom. Preferably a well decorated bedroom in another country. Living with adult children or other familia in the house make holidays more intense. It's the family reunion where no one leaves. You find yourself drinking glasses of Alka Seltzer rather than champagne.

Conversations between post-parental adults and returning adult children during celebrations should go like this: "Did you eat today?"

"Yeah."

"Got a roof over your head? Indoor plumbing?"

"Yeah."

"Okay, then, happy birthday." (Or whatever special day being hosted.)

They don't get it.

8

A Room of One's Own

Open space is highly overrated. I should know, I don't have any.

My dining-room-slash-office is cramped with enough books and papers to fill a large multi-conglomerate office building. I can't fit any more into the ten-by-fourteen-foot area since it houses an oak dining room table and twelve years worth of taxes, receipts, photos, and a collection of antiquated Egyptology books. My husband swears these musty tomes, picked up over the years from used bookstores everywhere, are my inheritance. The man who welcomed a houseful of returning adult children is the same man who tied up my retirement in books that say the same boring things over and over. Books about a handful of dead people with strange unpronounceable names, a few square miles of sand along a muddy river in the middle of no where, and dozens of ruins dotting the barren landscape and catacombing underneath.

One of the basic resources you lose when adult children move home is space. Whole rooms disappear behind closed doors, closets bulge from additional baggage, junk, and historical trinkets brought back by the twenty-something. Decorative shelves, once holding nothing but a few ornamental knick-knacks, start to sag in the middle from doing double duty as necessary holders for multiple people's hygiene products in the same household. Nooks and crannies (sounds like a rock 'n roll group) no longer exist, as every inch of available space is filled with someone's personal items.

Loss of space can be damaging to the psyche and the soul. Whole journals of medicine are written about the cause and effect of claustrophobia, and when Boomerangs invade their native homeland you get acute suffocation. If you've gotten used to the wide-open planes of Montana where you can stretch your legs without bumping your shins on something, and suddenly you're thrown into the heart of New York City at rush hour, your body is going to react. It's not a pretty sight.

Once again you're a victim of too few bathrooms, where you have to take a number for hygiene participation. Adult children monopolize the bathroom for eons with hair care and personal grooming routines that rival the beauty schedules of Tammy Faye Baker. You were this close to setting up his and hers bathrooms in an empty nest house. Picture moving hubby with his stacks of car and boat magazines out of your own domain and into the kids' former bathroom—being able to redecorate the room into a peaceful salon of lotus blossom colors and candles.

Okay, don't, it's too depressing. The CNS decorating theme is three sets of hair dryers, four different kinds of hair products, and a layer of wet towels for carpeting.

Once my kids grew up and out of the house I dreamt of closet space that didn't have to double as the North Pole and Santa's store room or the Easter Bunny's hidden nest of goodies during the year. That didn't happen, did it? There is no inch of closet space currently in my house that three different people don't have claim to, with all their stuff piled together. This alone should be grounds for combat pay. Crowding too many people into one house and abusing closet space is insane and dangerous.

One closet acts as part toy chest, holding action figure overloads and part sports locker for various sporting apparatus, stacks and wads of clothes under size 14 for short people smushed in the middle. Baseball, hockey sticks, footballs and cleats are mingled in the dark recesses with Power Rangers and radio-controlled cars in a closet meant for nothing more than a few hanging clothes and a couple of pair of shoes.

What are empty nesters whining about? They have full and complete access to every closet in their house. Can you imagine? You could have a blue closet where everything you own that's blue could be stored with no wrinkling and shoving, another that held all your beige stuff. Sheer bliss. You could organize, be methodical, separate and find whatever you wanted, whenever you wanted.

The scary part is I usually know where everything is in this over-stuffed shoe box of a house. No matter how many people move in and out I can pretty much find the birth certificates or the photo of the dog when he was just a puppy.

All I want is a counter top that doesn't have to be waded through like climbing Mt. Everest. Every flat surface in my house holds someone's life papers or the latest stack of clean laundry or last week's dirty laundry, with a few piles of remote controls for the three dozen different systems each adult keeps bringing into the house.

Returning adult children take up space—precious, wonderful space. They breathe your air and use up the resources of water and heat. Each one comes with car loads of life junk and treasures. They cram as much as they can into your domain and the rest is off to the rental storage unit. Remember, I said make the owner your best friend, you're going to need him for a long time.

Children expand when they first go out into the real world. They collect dogs and cats of their own and expect to bring them with them when they come back. They have bigger cars that hold more boxes and cartons of their own collectibles. There's the baseball card collection that has to be displayed where once you used to have blank wall space. Or the posters of who-knows-what that can't be crumpled up and stored are now plastered on the wallpaper you once picked out when these adult children were young and yours to raise.

You start buying futons by the dozen, and placing them around the house to cover sleepovers by the friends of the Boomerangs and their descendants. I love that word, descendants. Reminds me of Munchkinland in the *Wizard of Oz* where the mayor declared a day of independence, when the wicked witch of the East was killed. Sounds like my house, all the munchkins and their descendants. Remember the babies waking up in the nest outside the houses? See? *They* had the right idea from the get-go. Leave the children outside.

Virginia Wolfe talked about having a room of one's own in relation to writing. I say every American woman should be allowed her own room, a sanctuary of peace and quiet, a place for relaxing and recuperating. Maybe there's hope.

No matter how many square feet of living space I have, my aura attracts the clutter and piles of stuff to fill it up. I carry around a purse most men can't lift. My twenty-six pound satchel comes equipped with a small pharmacy, stationery store, Gramma's toy shop and enough plastic identification cards to melt into a life-sized Venus Di Milo. Why does every store and establishment need to give me a piece of bendable plastic with a barcode or magnetic strip? Did someone forget to tell me to invest in a magnetic strip company a couple of years ago? Someone is making a killing out there.

On the floor in the entry way where I keep my purse are a variety of bags, totes, and carry-on luggage. One is used for my writing group, one is used for work, and I'm not sure I remember what the other three are for. I'd never make it as a homeless person. I'd be trying to pull a train of three or four shopping carts down the street wherever I went. Clutter and chaos follow me, growing in the dark when I'm not looking.

To get a little elbow room and floor space, I tried to volunteer as a jurist on the OJ Simpson trial back in the Nineties. As soon as I heard rumors the panel of jurors might be sequestered for a long length of time, I sent my resume, an 8x10 glossy, and pleading cover letter of "pick me, pick me." Can you imagine? Those people were sheltered away from crowds and their own families with fresh towels magically arriving every day in the bathrooms and someone else making their beds. Okay, maybe they had to have one roommate. Hey, one is tolerable. In my house, it's more like half a dozen.

My house is so crowded, I resent the Christmas tree coming in during the month of December. It takes up a ton of floor space forcing me to clear a corner of the living room and where do you think that stuff goes? Right, in a closet.

My mailbox isn't even my own, I share it with three or four different last names. The duplicates of junk mail frighten the dog when they spill out like the girl in the Exorcist movie spewing pea soup. The mail carrier has given up deciding who is and who isn't living here any more and delivers whatever is in the sack for our street. Our whole street. He knows we'll sort it out, we have to anyway to find who gets what. There are more of us than him, our man power is cheaper.

I refuse to go out and buy the next larger size mailbox. Doesn't that seem like encouragement to fill it up even more? It's just giving up, a sign showing the world, yes, there are too many people in my house, and I'm too weak to enforce a deadline to kick them out.

I've tried sitting outside in the dead of winter to get a little solitude. No bugs, no spiders; but, dang, suddenly the grandkids think they need to learn how to play ice hockey using my shins as one of the goals. You tell them to go play outside and you get ninety-nine reasons why it isn't going to happen. Step outside yourself for solitude and they mob you going through the door. No one inherited my I-need-to-be-alone genes.

I try getting up before the crack of dawn and somebody is usually just getting in from a night of frivolity. No time or place can a human being be alone in this square footage of landscape and stucco. (Or siding. I guess I don't have a stucco house any more. I used to own one, back when the kids grew up; I thought I was in the home stretch for post-parenting solitude.)

A formal living room taunted me in mockery about my dreams when we first bought the stucco house. Oh the parties we would have there, the spaciousness of it all. Then it became an apartment for my mom. And when the adult daughter moved in, it also became a nursery for the baby.

We moved out before it could ever be restored to its original glory. It had cathedral ceilings and a fireplace. Such potential for a fun entertainment area.

I get a room of my own at work. Well, it's not a room, not even a cubicle, more like a few square feet I share with other co-workers. But it seems like a room of my own. The Monday blues hit me when the time clock says everyone should leave the office for the evening. I hate that part. I stall, I make up last minute projects or duties, anything to keep from going home. My boss is beginning to think a shoehorn is needed to force me out of my chair each day. He doesn't have insurance coverage for employees living on the premises. I wouldn't take up much room, with a roll away bed stored under the counter. There is a bathroom and microwave available. Works for me.

The late Princess Diana spent long hours over her last years trying to educate the world about abandoned land mines in third world countries. They're invisibly buried a few inches underground, causing horrendous devastation in seconds when triggered. The articles and photographs of her travels and commitment are ingrained in my mind and my heart. Her cause was and is a noble one as her sons have picked up the challenge to continue bringing this plight to the attention of the rest of us, until all the mines are carefully and painstakingly removed.

The above paragraph is to let you know I do understand the seriousness of abandoned land mines in the world. Do not send the publisher sacks of angry mail when I whine that CNS homes are also riddled with hidden land mines of a very different sort. Note the word different—yes, I think I can whine about this, I'm a redhead.

No foundation under the home is safe when adult children return. The bathroom, the living room, and even the kitchen hold invisible explosives in each square foot area, ready to incinerate any plan or schedule ahead of you.

Rushing to get ready for an important presentation at work and finding the bathroom door locked is a mine explosion. Once you get in a bathroom and find there is no more hot water and the deodorant container is empty are crippling land mines two and three. You dig through your closet knowing your forest green suit should be hanging there—but find nothing—ka-boom number four. See how your morning is going? You can duck and weave your way through the house and bodies thinking today you'll make it without problems, when suddenly a land mine explodes in your face.

As soon as you wake up in the morning, make sure you're wearing your identifying dog tags, and slip out from under the covers quietly. Your mission is to make it through the day alive. Don't get cocky out there, it's not safe. Keep your thoughts and wit about you as you scramble, finding a safe place of your own to stand to get ready for the day.

Protect yourself moving through the house. Hold your arm up over your eyes as you enter the den. Don't look at the gorgeous overstuffed couch you bought last year already decorated in soda and food stains along both arm rests with seat cushions torn and sagging from television marathons. Land mines. Or the fact that the Boomerang's cat has used the side panel for a scratching post. Another land mine.

They invade every square inch. No room in the house is safe from their clutter and presence. You never know when you'll step down and explode another mine. Your coffee table starts to reflect a battlefield, the life and times of a Generation-X on steroids, as it's covered in magazines with titles like *Studs Now* or *Wall Street Goes Hollywood*.

Be brave.

Seek shelter in various foxholes with names like Marriott and Holiday Inn. Accept a room key with what strength you have left, and let yourself into a room of your own. Even if you have to give it back in the morning.

9

The More the Merrier

Crowded Nest Syndrome, like many pseudo syndromes of the 21st Century, is not fatal. I don't mean to frighten you into cardiac arrest if one night your adult child shows up at your doorstep with suitcases in hand. CNS can be endured; even lived through successfully with the right amount of support from your friends and your pharmacist. It's a change of outlook or perspective on your part. If you can't move away from 'em, live with 'em.

Think of it as a new game plan, a different playbook in the rough and tumble contact sport of raising children. It's double overtime and the fans have left the stadium, but you're still playing. It is doable. You regroup, adjust, look around, and realize it's not the end of the world, just a few ripples or white caps in your pond.

With reality TV so popular many people think the rule of survival has become not who is right, but who hasn't been voted off the island. I say the Crowded Nest Syndrome is just the opposite, it's who and how many have been voted onto the island, and realizing many times your vote doesn't count. Fate gets a vote, unavoidable crisis may get a vote, oops and oh-no's get a vote, but you're just there to tally the results and get out of the way of the front door.

Make the best of the crowded situation. Serving rats on a stick isn't going to get them to move out any sooner. They'll accept your challenge and raise the bar to scenes straight out of *Fear Factor*. I don't need to watch these shows, I live them. The episodes of *Survivor* showing a group of people snarling and sniping at each other for food have nothing on my daily existence in crowded land here at home. The youngest learn quickly to grab and swallow the choicest bits of food or candy before the rest of the adults get their hands on them. Crawling on their bellies to find the last Hershey Kiss that rolled under the couch is their idea of winning the top prize. Course they fight the dog for it, and win only if it's beyond the reach of his front paw.

What's the other program where couples race across the world to an unknown destination? I can top that show any weekend at our house, as the adult children pair off to race against the parents for the last Diet Coke, the last roll of toilet paper, or the keys to the only car still working. Who-ever wakes up first has access to the most. You'd think that's a good thing for someone like me who wakes up at the crack of dawn. But adult children tend to stay up all night and, therefore, can win the morning caffeine fix because they just walked into the house at daybreak.

Whether you're living in episodes of reality TV or the *Simpson's*, keep breathing. A new season will turn up and maybe your reality show will be cancelled from lack of interest. The more things change the more they stay the same.

Speaking of new seasons, the daughter presented us with another little guy this year. Don't ask, it's a soap opera story all on its own. The little guy is cute and healthy, and has all the adults wrapped around his little finger. (I'll stop complaining in about twenty years or so.)

My next book will be titled "My Three Grandsons," and we'll turn it into a hilarious television sitcom re-make with a snappy toe-tapping theme song like the original *My Three Sons*. Another grandson. I don't feel like Fred McMurray, though fortunately, I do seem to have his same level of calmness. Mine is Prozac induced, his came through script rehearsals and going home after the show. I should look for a financial sponsor for my own side-splitting sit-com about three grandsons pulling their ancient grandma three different directions every week; each episode wrapping up neatly in less than thirty minutes with a happy ending.

Who should write the theme song for me? Elton John? Randy Newman? Something catchy that sticks in your mind as badly as "don't worry, be happy" kind of thing. No one's going to believe the concept, but it will warm the hearts of those having to endure their own family situation comedies of the more the merrier.

The dog is ecstatic. A new baby living with us means a new rugrat tossing Cheerios down from the highchair. Oh, yeah. A slow moving vehicle in plastic Pampers dripping toast crusts and slobbery cracker crumbs all over the floor, a new best friend to break into the concept of sharing everything you eat, whether you want to or not. The dog loves these little guys we keep bringing home until they're old enough to fend off the food-related affections.

A new baby. The house stretches and bends a little more, squeezing in a brand new bassinet and changing table. The good news is when babies start out in the world, they don't take up much physical space. I now understand the concept from our ancestors of babies sleeping in a drawer of the dresser. A house only has so much square footage, and the more people and possessions you cram into the space, the less room for new products.

Generations-past newborns did quite well sleeping in a deep drawer with blankets or towels for comfort. Doesn't Japan have hotels where you rent a cubicle not much bigger than an adult sized dresser drawer for sleeping? Same idea.

The weekly groceries again contain a can of formula, a package of diapers and tushy wipes. The array of toiletries picked up at Target or Wal-Mart for the family contain diaper rash products and no tear formula shampoo. How easily another being comes into the pandemonium and finds its niche and elbow room.

They start out small so they can stretch the fabric of family hearth and heart as they grow. You're used to having them in the scheme of things and naturally start carving out an extra chair at the table, a bigger car with more seating capacity. Kids happen.

🚲

Baby boomer grandparents are adaptable creatures; we're the original Play dough generation. Leave us alone with the grandchildren for a while, and we evolve into multi-tasking over-achievers. Post-parental units enduring a second generation of standing in line at fast food places; that's us waiting for pressed meat and fattening fries. Short people tug at our hearts demanding a toy with every meal and a chance to run off the adrenaline of life and sugar at plastic play lands. Nothing like donating your paycheck toward the happiness of the grandkids, and the hardening of your arteries at the same time; no way you can sit in these international establishments time after time and not eat the fries whether you're under the Golden Arches or at BK. The fries'll getcha.

My golden years were supposed to be filled with Sunday champagne brunches at the beach with cloth napkins and adult conversations. Maybe not caviar and capers on toast sort of affair, but I definitely know delicious arrays of delights tempting any palette would be spread across multiple tables in a cavernous room. Where someone quietly takes away your empty plate and brings you a fresh clean one with a smile. Instead in my post-parenting years I get paper napkins and plastic ketchup packets.

You learn to read the newspaper and concentrate on world events with noise levels around you reaching dangerous decibels. Children of all sizes and shapes running, screaming around you, their screeches reaching maximum penetration when echoing through huge floor-to-ceiling plastic human-sized hamster tubing. Stories of war and politics lose their bloodletting edge when a generation of fresh-faced curly tops dash past you squealing in utter delight in notes that can shatter glass. You'll note drinks only come in paper cups; there's a reason for this.

I'm normal, I confess. I had dreams, once the kids were off to college or on their own, of whole weekends reading in solitude, maybe a soft concerto playing on the radio, maybe the windows open and birds outside singing in natural harmony. Instead I've learned to write out my bills and personal letters cooped up in a molded chair, at Ronald's playhouse, explaining laws of physics to the three-year-old that what goes up must come down. If you climb up the maze of yellow, blue, and green hamster tubing, you will come down. Somewhere. Whether it's the short baby slide or the three-story curved one, or bribing someone else's child to go in after yours when they panic halfway through the equipment, the child will come back.

Don't bother trying to leave early from these establishments, make yourself as comfortable as possible. I sit across from the used-to-be youngest and hear things like "When my hair is sweaty, and my tummy hurts, then I'll tell you I want to go home." There it is there.

My young gym-addicted doctor tells me I should do more exercise. He hasn't seen me doing the fifty-yard dash in nine seconds to a restroom at McDonalds when the preschooler got a bloody nose dodging his brother and ran into the edge of the playground equipment. I can carry an extra thirty-five pounds for an hour on my right hip over the distance of two grocery stores while pushing a shopping cart they refuse to sit in. And this young soap-opera doctor wants me to do more exercise? Maybe a bitter empty nester might need more exercise with nothing better to do than whine at the rest of us for taking up too many chairs. Me? Fer-getta about it.

My hearing fails me once in a while; most people think it's due to an aging body. The ringing in my ears is caused by the same Backstreet Boys' song played 6,892 times over and over making it difficult to hear anyone on *Sixty Minutes*. Their words blur together to form a continuous chorus of "rock your body." I watch Morley Schaffer's lips move, but I swear he sounds like the lead singer of the Baha Men by the time it crosses the room.

No, we won't retire as early as planned. We're deep in debt, sticky with sugar-coated kisses, and the calendar is marked with school programs and Cub Scout meetings. There's a whole group of Crowded Nesters with us.

We're not alone out here on the fifty yard line of life. Not only are more kids moving back to Mom's—but a few more Enron and WorldCom corporate disasters, and we'll all have to move in with each other. Working toward an early retirement isn't a possibility for many baby boomers any more. Responsibilities are draining what little resources we have at an alarming rate.

We spend leisure time at Home and Garden shows for ideas in expanding our four-bedroom house with $1.98 in our checking account. Scary, isn't it? Maybe if I add more mirrors everywhere the illusion of space will appear. It already feels like a Fun House at the carnival, I might as well decorate like one. No cozy retirement cottage in our future—I look at ways of making the living room bigger where we won't have to take a number to sit on the couch. Or another idea is adding a few feet to the master bedroom. If I'm spending extra time in there watching my shows and stealing some solitude—let me have a little elbowroom, please. I'd like a rocking chair recliner, too, while I'm dreaming. Something I can curl up in to read and wonder what lies ahead with the newest grandson added to the troops.

The old saying is the apple doesn't fall far from the tree. Have you seen most varieties of apple trees? I resent the implication I am an ugly, knarled, disjointed tree, or that I came from one. A city girl all my life, apples came from the grocery store. The romantic thoughts of huge luscious apple trees, the warm-hearted legend of Johnny Appleseed, and songs like "Don't sit under the apple tree…" are how I envisioned these mighty trees.

I'm driving down a winding road on my way to work and pass all these stark stick figure trees that come autumn I find out are apple trees, and it depresses the heck out of me. The apple doesn't fall far from the tree, oh, thank you, very much. Wicked looking, scraggly things bearing bright red fruit. In the dusk driving home these trees growing by the side of the road look like the evil witch in *Snow White*. I think Disney Imagineers had them in mind when they drew her. The branches look like her arms reaching out to hurt you as you drive under them. The apple in the story represented a symbol of evil, too.

It takes two trees to make the fruit, doesn't it? Hello—not in my crazy-branched tree. There are hundreds of types of apples out in the world, how come I get the spoiled ones in various sizes? Can I exchange a few of them? My luck I'd get Snow White's poisoned one.

The apple seeds continue generation after generation, though, despite everything else—it's the grandkids you get attached to when the Boomerangs move back. The beauty in the next generation of apple blossoms will get you every time. The newest grandson proves my theory, as he wrinkles his brow and curls up his arms in odd pointed fashion like branches of a tree, drawing his long fingers up into twig shapes. Yep, that's a twig off my old tree.

Remember, if nothing else, *Empty Nest* was just a sitcom on television. During the Eighties it was cute when Kristy McNichol played a cop and lived at home with her father and neurotic older sister. It's not cute when you're the parent trying to have a nice quiet, happily-ever-after once the kids are supposed to be grown and on their own in the big wide world and they come back. Who knew our kids were absorbing the wrong message from the show? Could we have imagined back then how many were going to move back home?

None of the post-parental issues I deal with wrap up neatly in a half-hour, let alone leaving time for commercials. No laugh tracks are heard in the background during the chaos and escapades; no one applauds my stellar efforts to keep peace and sanity at the end of each exhausting evening. The characters seem to play out different episodes and storylines, yet there isn't an audience rating their performance.

Maybe we can file a class action suit and sue the former producers of *Empty Nest* for brain washing the younger generation into thinking it was an acceptable concept without showing them the burden in dollars and cents the girls put on their father's budget. Maybe a sadistic tech added subliminal messages to the show while our kids were watching like "You will return home at twenty-three. You will return home at twenty-three."

If we play the sit-com episodes backwards, will it tell us Paul McCartney, er, Kristy McNichol is dead? Boomerangs probably don't know about this myth. Can you play a CD backwards? I was never able to play my eight-track tape version of rock music backward.

When I was a little girl, I wanted to be a hermit when I grew up, live alone in a deep forest, taking care of furry woodland animals, leaving food out for cute little squirrels, and make friends with Bambi and a wise old owl. Two of my favorite books I devoured over and over back then were *Freckles*, about a young boy living and working in a forest, and *The Boxcar Children* where four orphans lived in a deserted train car in the woods.

Did my career of choice come from being the original latch key kid in my neighborhood? I enjoyed waking up alone in the house where both parents left for work at the crack of dawn (my siblings were adults with their own families.) I got ready for school and came home afterward to a house that was all mine. Even then I wasn't a great cook, but my mom appreciated my efforts to start dinner.

I felt like an only child most of my childhood. Being umpteen years older than I am, my two brothers and sister moved out early from my parents' nest. By having an empty house as a child, does that mean I don't get to have one now? Who screwed up my life schedule?

No surprise my favorite Disney animation movie was *Sleeping Beauty*, which had a great part in the middle where Aurora as a baby is called Briar Rose and gets to live in the woods with three fairies. Is that heaven or what? So where am I now? No fairies, that's for sure, in an over crowded four-bedroom house with multiple generations. Whose idea is this? Is someone up there laughing away at this twist to my happy ending? I can take care of this many people, but why do I have to? Cuz Momma raised me to take care of things.

I should be happy I made it to the forest at least. I drive forty-five minutes along a winding road under heavy branches of lush leaves to work each day. My commute is my only peace and quiet. Otherwise, my home life's three or four televisions blaring, six people trying to talk all at once about their day, and large four-legged animals wanting scraps of attention, too.

As a little girl I wanted to be a hermit. When I got older I wanted to move to Canada with the draft dodgers, change my name, disappearing into a conglomerate of people. Alone in a crowd. I know they weren't drafting women, I wanted the escape excuse. Where am I today? Surrounded by too many bodies, healthy loud bodies, inflicting their needs and wants on me. So much for years of planning.

Mt. Rainier sits guard over us on the horizon, proud, tall, impressive. Picture postcard looking. Yet climbers challenge its height every year. They force themselves up the face of the mountain, battling their fears and pushing the envelope. Some don't come down. They don't think about the fear, they go for the thrill, taking each minute at a time.

This family is my Mt. Rainier, it's my challenge to endure, to think, to keep my wits about me all the time. Watch where I put my feet for strength, grasp for hand holds where none exist. You cling to minimal edges by adrenaline and spit. My protective safety gear is my heart and my friends. One day at a time, one foot in front of the other.

It's hard to breathe inside the house sometimes, where oxygen is thin when a three-year-old is sucking most of it out of the atmosphere. His mouth never closes, the constant volume out of his tiny orifice is astounding. He must gulp huge amounts of oxygen in his sleep, because the rest of the day is set in releasing carbon dioxide in a stream of chatter, whining, and repeating himself.

Mountain climbers bring tanks of oxygen with them knowing the high altitudes will cause light headedness and blackouts. No one warned me I needed my own equipment, didn't leave me a list of what to bring into the future. I think you should be able to go into Target and pick up a few extra tanks of pure oxygen to get you through the toughest parts.

We (the collective we—all past generations included) have created this mixed up world. A world where pizza orders can arrive at your house faster than an ambulance. Where lemon juice from a fruit-shaped squeeze bottle is made with artificial flavorings but dishwashing liquid is made with real lemons. Forwarded Internet emails are famous for sending out lists of "can you believe" to remind us how bizarre and irrational normal has become. Like the fact that hot dogs come in packages of ten but hot dog buns are in packages of eight. Maybe Boomerangs are the extra hot dog buns of the family.

We raised our children as best we could and tried to send them out into the world where a bottle of children's cold medicine has a label "Do not drive a car or operate machinery after taking this medicine." I'm sorry, I didn't know we needed fine print to remind us not to give the keys to the minivan to any under age kid on cold medicine. We make them wear helmets and knee pads, shin guards and elbow pads to go outside to play. Is it any wonder in this over protected scheme of things our adult children are coming home in droves?

Crowded Nest Syndrome is not for the faint of heart. When you fell in love and looked at the world through new rose-colored 3-D glasses, anything was possible, love conquered all. Having a house full of overgrown children and grandchildren is the test of faith to a relationship.

If you love him, you endure, you go on. Keep journals of notes for yourself as the ultimate pay back later in your retirement years, if you ever get to have any.

You couldn't imagine when you walked down the aisle on your wedding day with friends and family smiling and crying around you what was ahead. You wore this spotless gown, high heels, and veil feeling on top of the world. Where is that cute ceramic couple sitting on the top layer of wedding cake now?

Oh, that's right, we're the ones in fast food Happyland USA reading the newspaper waiting for the grandkiddles to come out of the plastic hamster tubes.

The recordings of Mozart playing at our wedding have been replaced with boy bands and countless renditions of the Itsy Bitsy spider, who never gives up trying to make it up the water spout. That's us. Never give up. Never give up hope, never give up ground. Never give out the pin number to your ATM card.

You *can* survive Crowded Nest Syndrome.

About the Author

Kathleen Shaputis is alive and well living in the Pacific Northwest with her husband, Bob, and a cast of characters too numerous to mention.

Kathleen is well experienced in the headline lifestyles of the baby boomer generation; her own life mimics a daily soap opera of catch phrases and hot topics.

The Crowded Nest Syndrome is Kathleen's first self-published book.

Photo by Zone V

Kathleen is also the author of *Grandma Online: A Grandmother's Guide to the Internet* (Ten Speed Press, 2001.) A humorous guide of over six hundred web sites with personal experiences related to the joys and concerns of grandmothers and fairy grandmothers the world over, *Grandma Online* encourages intergenerational usage of the Internet, creating a crossover readership.

In addition to her day job, Kathleen enjoys speaking to various groups on CNS awareness, writing, publishing and the Internet. She welcomes any excuse to stay out of the house a few more minutes.

To request Kathleen Shaputis as a speaker for your organization or conference, please send a query letter with dates and location to Clutter Fairy Publishing, P. O. Box 11056, Olympia, WA 98508-1056.

Clutter Fairy Publishing

Order Form

To order an autographed copy of The Crowded Nest Syndrome,
send your request with check or money order to:

Clutter Fairy Publishing
P. O. Box 11056
Olympia WA 98508-1056

— *or* —

Go to www.CrowdedNestSyndrome.com to place credit card orders

	PRICE	QUANTITY	SUBTOTAL
The Crowded Nest Syndrome Surviving the Return of Adult Children	$13.95		
Shipping and Handling For the first book	$2.50		
Additional Shipping and Handling For each additional book	$1.50		
		TOTAL	

Booksellers, corporations, and libraries should place their orders
with Independent Publishers Group (800) 888-4741